THE
HIDDEN PLACES

of

South Wales

*Gwent, Glamorgan, Pembrokeshire, Dyfed
and South Powys*

ACKNOWLEDGEMENTS

This book would not have been compiled without the dedicated help of the following:
Elaine, Adele - Administration. Albert, Les & Graham Sarah - Artists. Bob, Jody,
Simon, Lou, Jim, Clare, Adele & Debbie - Research. Leon & Chris- DTP.

All have contributed to what we hope is an interesting, useful and enjoyable publication.

OTHER TITLES IN THIS SERIES

The Hidden Places of Devon and Cornwall
The Hidden Places of East Anglia
The Hidden Places of The Cotswolds
The Hidden Places of Hampshire and Isle of Wight
The Hidden Places of the Lake District and Cumbria
The Hidden Places of Lancashire and Cheshire
The Hidden Places of Northumberland and Durham
The Hidden Places of North Wales
The Hidden Places of Notts, Derby and Lincolnshire
The Hidden Places of Somerset, Avon and Dorset
The Hidden Places of the South East
The Hidden Places of South Wales
The Hidden Places of Scotland
The Hidden Places of Thames and Chilterns
The Hidden Places of Yorkshire and Humberside

Printed and bound by Guernsey Press, Channel Islands
© M & M PUBLISHING LTD
Tryfan House, Warwick Drive, Hale, Altrincham, Cheshire. WA15 9EA

Introduction

THE HIDDDEN PLACES is designed to be an easily used book, taking you, in this instance, on a gentle meander through the beautiful countryside of South Wales. However, our books cover many counties and will eventually encompass the whole of the United Kingdom. We have combined descriptions of the well-known and enduring tourist attractions with those more secluded and as yet little known venues, easy to miss unless you know exactly where you are going.

We include hotels, inns, restaurants, various types of accomodation, historic houses, museums, gardens and general attractions throughout this fascinating area, together with our research on the local history. For each attraction there is a line drawing and a brief description of the services offered. A map at the beginning of each chapter shows you each area, with many charming line drawings of the places we found on our journey.

We do not include firm prices or award merits. We merely wish to point out *The Hidden Places* that hopefully will improve your holiday or business trip and tempt you to return. The places featured in this book will we are sure, be pleased if you mention that it was The Hidden Places which prompted you to visit.

THE HIDDEN PLACES

OF

South Wales

CONTENTS

CHAPTER ONE

Gwent.

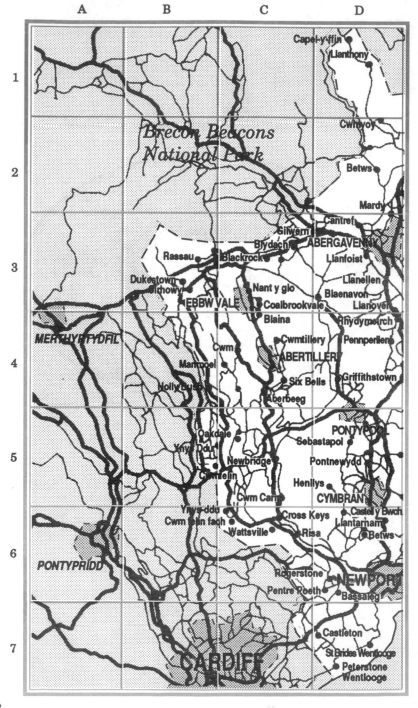

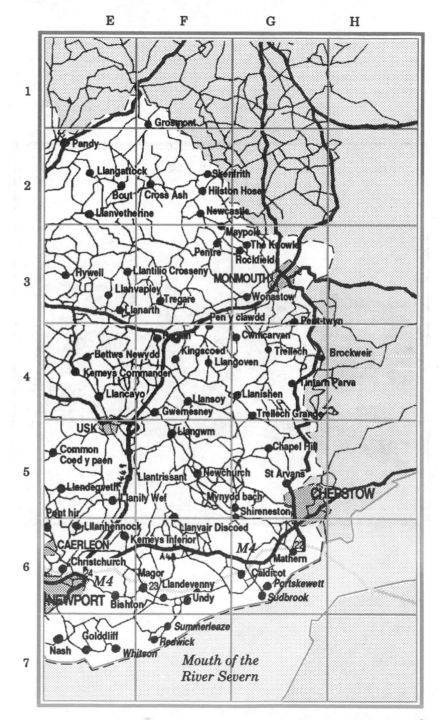

E F G H

1

Grosmont

Pandy

2

Llangattock

Skenfrith

Bout Cross Ash Hilston Hose

Llanvetherine Newcastle

Maypole

The Knowle

Pentre Rockfield

3

Hywell Llantilio Crosseny MONMOUTH

Llanvapley Wonastow

Tregare

Llanarth Pen y clawdd Pen-twyn

Dingen Cwmcarvan

Bettws Newydd Kingscoed Trellech Brockweir

4

Kemeys Commander Llangoven

Tintern Parva

Llancayo Llansoy Llanishen

Gwernesney Trellech Grange

USK Llangwm

Common Chapel Hill

Coed y paen

5

Llantrissant Newchurch St Arvans

Llandegveth

Llanily Wef Mynydd bach CHEPSTOW

Pent hir Shireneston

Llanhennock Llanvair Discoed

CAERLEON Kemeys Inferior M4

6

Christchurch A4 Mathern

Magor Caldicot

M4 23 Llandevenny Portskewett

NEWPORT Bishton Undy Sudbrook

Summerleaze

Golddliff Redwick

Nash Whitson

7 *Mouth of the*
River Severn

3

Chepstow Castle.

CHAPTER ONE

Gwent.

Our first glimpse of Wales came as we approached the magnificent **Severn Bridge** along the M4 motorway. It's more than one bridge, really, for it crosses both the River Severn and the River Wye. Once across the bridge we noticed the sign *'Croeso i Cymru '* - Welcome to Wales, adorned with the red dragon, the Welsh national symbol. We were now in the county of Gwent better known, perhaps, as Monmouthshire, its name before county boundary reorganisation in the 1970s. Moves are, however, afoot to return to the old county name. Nevertheless Gwent is a fascinating area with two distinct sides to its character. Although mainly a rural county, it includes within its boundaries part of the old industrial coal bearing valleys. But the overall impression is one of a peaceful, pastoral area where farming is the chief occupation. These were certainly our first impressions on crossing the Severn Bridge. The borderlands are peaceful today, but in medieval times they were in the front line between warring English and Welsh forces. Many of Gwent's towns sprung up around the castles built by successive English monarchs along a key military border.

Chepstow, our first stop in Wales, is one such town. Built on the banks of the River Wye, it has the distinction of being based around the first castle in Britain to be constructed of stone. The well preserved fortress, on a crag overlooking the river, was founded just after the Norman Conquest by William FitzOsbern, and later belonged to the Norman Strongbow, one of the powerful Marcher Lords (and, incidentally, the man who conquered Ireland in the 12th century). Opposite the castle is a museum with exhibits of local history. The medieval town walls enclose narrow streets, and the main road is straddled by a 14th century town gate which adds further to the town's charming historic character while at the same time being something of a traffic hazard! Chepstow is a bustling little town with many interesting shops to browse around.

A place we would reccomend during your browse is just down the hill from the church in the centre of Chepstow, **Ned Heywood's Pottery and Gallery.** Ned is a highly skilled potter with an individual approach and a countrywide reputation. The Gallery, in Lower Church Street, houses a collection of his work and the striking first impression is one of classic shapes and beautiful soft green and blue glazes. Ned welcomes visitors to his workshop. Only here can they appreciate the full range of his ceramics, including a series of Victorian pub sculptures, with superb architectural detail. Above the workshop he runs a gallery which shows a varied programme of work by leading U.K. potters and artists.

Ned Heywood Workshop Gallery ,Chepstow 0291 624836 Map Ref:5G

Chepstow Racecourse, on the northern approaches to the town, is the largest in Wales, and after a day at the races or shopping, where better to relax than at the end of Chepstow High Street in the lovely setting of Beaufort square, **The Beaufort Hotel**, a superb Georgian building offering first class accommodation at surprisingly reasonable prices.

The Beaufort Hotel, Chepstow 0291 622497 (Fax: 0291 627389) Map Ref: 5G

This former coaching inn was the traveller's lodge for the ancient Anglo-Saxon monastic settlement and has undergone sensitive restoration and refurbishment by its present owners to provide every modern comfort whilst retaining its original character. There are 22 attractively furnished guest rooms, twenty of which have en-suite facilities and in the elegant Georgian surroundings of the restaurant, you can choose from an excellent and varied menu which is accompanied by an extensive wine list.

Alternatively on the edge of town, close to Offas Dyke, Wye Valley walks and just two minutes from the centre of the historic old town of Chepstow, standing opposite the Baptist church, **"Lantern House"** built prior to the 15th century, is also an art and craft material centre. The property, owned and restored by Anne Ross-Samson, stands on a site that has yielded flint stone tools and a Roman or earlier dice. The site later formed part of the monastery standing in the castle grounds, and was probably the guest house for the monastery, then surrounded by orchards producing apple and cherry ciders. The four double bedrooms are tastefully decorated and well-equipped and all diets are catered for with warm hospitality.

Lantern House, Chepstow 0291 622195 Map Ref: 5G

To the south of Chepstow but within easy reach of the town and its facilities, **Leechpool House** enjoys a peaceful rural setting with views over the Severn Estuary. **Portskewett,** meaning 'Port by the Woods', was once the major port of the kingdom of Gwent.

Victorian Farmhouse, Leechpool House, Portskewett 0291 423230 Map Ref: 6G

Built as a farmhouse in the late 1800s, the house was once occupied by a farmer, his wife and thirteen children. Nowadays, hosts Susan and Allen Langford offer bed and breakfast to their guests in a relaxed no-smoking atmosphere. The three bedrooms are all family sized with colour/satellite TV. The large garden has a well-equipped play area including a splash pool. The Langfords provide baby-sitting and laundry services for the benefit of parents. Snacks, refreshments and evening meals are available if required.

The countryside west of Chepstow is a delightful mixture of rolling hills, woods and farmlands. On the B4235 between Chepstow and Usk at **Shirenewton** is **The Huntsman Hotel,** where the hunt meets regularly and has amongst its members the show-jumper David Broome.

The Huntsman, owned by Mr and Mrs Moles is a friendly, well run hotel, where you can stay in one of the ten very comfortable and attractively furnished bedrooms, eight of which are en suite and all have colour television, tea/coffee making facilities and telephones. The restaurant and bar meals have become very popular and well known for miles around. It is common on a Sunday for them to serve two hundred meals. All the food is fresh and with the Moles' experience you can rest assured that you will be served with only the best. Outside there is a large seating area, which is very pretty with hanging baskets on the walls. The Huntsman is one of those places where everyone is welcome. Children are never seen to be a nuisance. It is only five to six miles from the Severn Bridge and the M4, and just three miles from Chepstow.

The Huntsman Hotel, Shirenewton 02917 521 Map Ref: 6G

From **Shirenewton** we decided to head through the lanes for the neighbouring village of **Wolvesnewton.** The hills around Wolvesnewton are an ideal retreat undisturbed by any signs of hustle and bustle, a perfect place to visit and stay. **The Model Farm Folk Museum** is a collection of unique farm buildings built by the Duke of

8

Beaufort in the 18th century, with views overlooking breathtaking countryside. You can get a feel for the humour of the Victorian era and agricultural history of the area in many of the exhibits. Children love the Quiz Trail that they can follow around the museum. The farm animals are a delight for all ages to see in such a lovely place. A craft shop sells memorabilia and you can watch craftsmen at work making toys such as rocking horses

For fine days there is an adventure playground and a picnic area but if the weather is being unkind to you then The Model Farm is still an excellent place to come to because there is so much to see inside and you can also indulge yourselves in the restaurant which is licensed and serves a delicious range of home cooked food throughout the day.

Model Farm Museum, Wolvesnewton 02915 231 Map Ref: 6G

In an isolated village lying in a hollow formed by the hills of Llangwm to the west and the Newchurch Range to the south, we found **Cwrt -y- Gaer**, where Sue and John Llewellyn have three self-catering apartments to let offering the chance to enjoy a quiet holiday away from it all. Ysgubor Uchaf, is approached up the old stone steps to a spacious luxury room with dining facilities. The kitchen area is well appointed with a cooker, fridge and all that is necessary. There is a double bedroom, twin beds and a bathroom with shower. Extra sleeping accommodation is available with the three seater sofa bed which converts into a double bed. Ysgubor Isaf also faces south and also sleeps four. It has a particularly spacious living room with dining area. Byre Cottage has been designed with easy access for the disabled. You can sleep four here comfortably.

Cwrt-y-Gaer, Wolvesnewton 02915 700 Map Ref: 6G

Nearby Wolvesnewton takes its name from a Norman family of the 13th century named Lupus (Wolf) of Lovel, who were lords here holding, at the service of a moiety, for a half knight's fee. Cwrt -y-

Gaer, which is a quarter of a mile to the west is believed to be the site of their manor house or castle and it may, possibly have been built on the site of a more ancient dwelling situated as it is on a mound of about an acre and a half surrounded by a moat on the west and south supplied with water from a spring.

For those looking for peace and quiet we found **Parsons Grove**, set in the most delightful countryside at **Earlswood** near Chepstow, a superbly renovated old house, parts of which date back as far as the 17th century. Welcoming hosts Ernie and Gloria Powell provide superb accommodation in two beautifully furnished en-suite guest rooms plus a well-appointed family annexe, each equipped with hot drinks facilities, colour TV, and radio. We have to say that the entire house is immaculate and the lounge has a super beamed ceiling and French doors opening onto a raised patio area overlooking the swimming pool. Guests are encouraged to use the pool, weather permitting, as well as the lovely conservatory which is magic in the morning and evening sunlight. Within the grounds of Parsons Grove, there are also three self-contained cottages, all furnished to an equally high standard and with provision for the disabled. To complete a stay here, what could be nicer than the party atmosphere of a barbecue by the swimming pool accompanied by Welsh wine from Ernie and Gloria's own vineyard!

Parsons Grove, Earlswood, Near Chepstow 02917 382 Map Ref: 5G

The next day, our first priority was a visit to that most beautiful of spots, **Tintern.** We made our way eastwards to the riverside village, which nestles amongst the wooded slopes of the lovely **Wye Valley**. The entire valley, from Chepstow to Monmouth, is an officially designated Area of Outstanding Natural Beauty. Tintern itself, of course, is famous for its ruined abbey as well as its glorious woodlands (they are especially beautiful in the autumn). The Cistercian house, now a majestic ruin, was founded in 1131 by Walter de Clare and was active until the Dissolution of the Monasteries by Henry VIII. It's easy to see why this abbey, in its splendid setting, inspired poetry from William Wordsworth and was painted by Turner.

Tintern's former railway station is now a Visitor Centre and a good source of information on what to see and where to walk in this lovely valley. Situated in the centre of Tintern village, **The Falls Guest House** is an unusual property which boasts a simply delightful waterfall which cascades some forty feet into a pool and then feeds a stream running through the four lawns of the garden.

Within these beautiful surroundings you will discover two types of accommodation; either bed and breakfast en-suite or a two-bedroom holiday flat which covers the whole top floor of the house. Exceptionally well-equipped the flat has a fully fitted kitchen complete with microwave, plus a separate lounge, dining room and bathroom. If you prefer, David and Nan Norris are friendly hosts who enjoy welcoming guests into their charming 18th century home and offer very comfortable accommodation with first class food, readily catering for vegans and vegetarians as required.

The Falls Guest House, Tintern 0291 689215 Map Ref: 4G

For a perfect day out for the whole family, **Abbey Mill** in Tintern is ideal. This was the original mill site of Tintern Abbey (founded in 1131) and has been amongst other things, a Corn, Woollen and Saw Mill during its varied history. Today the site houses two delightful shops, a tearoom and restaurant all managed by the same family who have been here in Tintern for three generations. Visitors can browse through a selection of quality clothing and gifts or choose from a wealth of local and British handcrafted products. Enjoy sitting by the mill pond and watch the fish or perhaps buy some rainbow trout to take home for tea. The Abbey Mill tearoom and restaurant are well-renowned for their exceptional value for money. Take some time and hire a Mountain Bike to explore the woods and country lanes, it's wonderful! Abbey Mill is worth stopping for.

Abbey Mill, Tintern 0291 689228 Map Ref: 4G

The Romans some fifteen hundred years ago introduced the vine to the Wye Valley and later the Cistercian monks of Tintern made wine on a south facing hill overlooking the abbey. So when Martin Rogers tackled the monumental task of transforming this wild Welsh hill and bringing it back to a vineyard, it was more than just a battle against nature. He has succeeded splendidly, and **Tintern Parva Vineyard** at Tintern Parva Farm is a credit to him.

To enjoy this vineyard experience take pass through Tintern and just after the Wye Valley Hotel you will come to Parva Farm, on your left. It is advisable to have sensible and comfortable footwear to enjoy the tour of the vineyards. For just £2.50 per head you will enjoy a most informative tour, including a lecture on the history of the Tintern Grape from vine to wine. You are able to taste the wines and if to your liking stock up your own wine cellar with purchases from the vineyard shop.

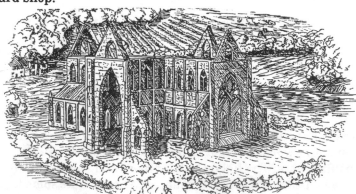

Tintern Parva Vineyard, Tintern 0291 689636 Map Ref: 4G

Tintern Abbey.

Valley House on Raglan Road in Tintern is a unique Georgian three storey house enjoying a delightful setting in the heart of the Angiddy Valley, one mile from Tintern Abbey. The home of Anne and Peter Howe, this is an exceptional establishment where you enjoy a hearty breakfast in the comfortable surroundings of the arched stone cellar, and retire at night to one of the delightfully furnished en-suite guest rooms.

The wooded surroundings provide excellent walking country, dotted with picnic places for your pleasure and Peter and Anne have a wealth of information about the industrial archaeology of the area to share with their guests, so they can best appreciate the beauty of this lovely hideaway in the Wye Valley.

Valley House, Tintern 0291 689652 Map Ref: 4G

Across the Wye Valley from Tintern we visited **Brockweir** were we found interesting places to detain the visitor. Turning off the **A466** towards Brockweir you will find a real gem at **Malthouse Pottery** immediately on your right after the Brockweir Inn crossroads. Proprietor Peter Naylor is a master craftsman who designs his own range of beautiful pots, with lovely greens and blues provided by mud from the river Wye which runs right outside. Housed within a 600 year old building originally built as an upper hall-house by the monks of Tintern Abbey. If you arrive on the right day you may see Peter at work in the undercroft, which, during the late 15th century was a malthouse where fine ale and cider were made. Today however, you can marvel at the simply delightful wine goblet sets, bowls, jugs and vases that Peter creates here.

14

Malthouse Pottery, Brockweir 0291 689291 Map Ref: 4G

In the heart of the village you will discover a delightful 400 year old hostelry, **The Brockweir Country Inn** which we mentioned above, backing onto the oldest Moravian church in England and only fifty yards from the River Wye.

Here a warm, friendly atmosphere is enhanced by old beams and a log fire. Children are welcome and there is a sheltered beer garden which provides the setting for regular summer barbecues. The bar boasts five regularly changing real ales and both the bar food and weekend restaurant menus are extensive and imaginative. For those wishing to stay there are three character rooms, one boasting a four poster bed.

The Brockweir Country Inn, Brockweir 0291 689548 Map Ref: 4G

Back down in the Wye Valley, the A466 winds it way up beside the river and towards our next port of call, the historic town of **Monmouth.** We made a small detour however, up to **Llandogo** where there are

15

good views of the valley from PenyFan, a wooded hill above Bigsweir Bridge. One of the last maypoles in Gwent was sited here, although nowadays it is down in the valley. Can you find it?

The Park House Tavern, Trellech 0600 860224 Map Ref: 4G

No luck? Well relax after your efforts by enjoying a peaceful roadside setting in the picturesque village of Trellech, at **The Park House Tavern** looking out over peaceful farmland and distant Welsh hills - a charming stopping-off point in any journey. Friendly host Bob Jenkins is an expert in livestock husbandry and Lesley, his wife, is a superb cook.

Together they make The Park House one of the finest hostelries in Gwent. In the 38-seater restaurant you can savour Lesley's fine homecooking, with specialities such as Welsh Faggots and super Ploughman's salads with over 20 different ingredients, plus Welsh steaks supplied by local farms. A popular local watering-hole, arrive early and join in the friendly banter, with no juke box or fruit machine to interrupt you.

The Village Green Restaurant, Trellech 0600 860119 Map Ref: 4G

The **Village Green Restaurant** in the heart of Trellech is owned by Bob and Jane Evans whose love for good food led them to open this charming place. Formerly a coaching inn, this lovely restaurant has excellent English and French cuisine, that has been mentioned in food guides. An a la carte menu is available or alternatively a brasserie with blackboard menu. The restaurant has covers for about twenty five people and will cater for children. All the dishes are cooked with fresh local market produce.

The Fountain Inn, at Trellech Grange is a lovely 17th century inn, once a watering hole for cattle drovers on their way from Monmouth to Chepstow market.

The Inn was even used by the local registrar as his office once a week to record events. Inside the bar is beamed and intimate, and offers, apart from the warmth of hospitality, a fine selection of ales, malt whiskeys, wine and bar meals. The restaurant, with a separate entrance from the pub specialises in traditional country dishes. Children are catered with sensible portions and the use of high chairs or booster seats if need be. The Fountain also has some simple but comfortable letting accommodation, as well as a certified caravan, discreetly tucked away in a field to one side.

Fountain Inn, Trellech Grange 0291 689303 Map Ref: 4G

Immediately left from the Fountain Inn you will find **The Smithy,** home of Elaine and Frank Barker who have totally renovated the Old Smithy into a friendly, comfortable Guest House. Frank is a retired woodwork teacher and has put his skills to making numerous pieces of furniture in the house including a beautiful carved dining table in oak complete with a set of chairs. Elaine cooks supremely well, substantial breakfasts, and evening meals by arrangement as well providing free packed lunches for those staying more than one night.

The Smithy Guest House, Trellech Grange 0600 860027 Map Ref: 4G

17

Those wishing a different setting in recognition of their efforts should try a 'hidden place' **The Trekkers**, a delightful log cabin pub which stands at the edge of The Narth forest, in an area of outstanding natural beauty. Run by Peter and Susan Flower, The Trekkers has a deserved reputation for superb homecooked food and fine Real Ales and wines. The lively atmosphere is reminiscent of a skiing resort, with European-style decor to match. The garden gazebo provides a stage for bands on 'al fresco' evenings, whilst the skittle alley provides hours of entertainment and for anyone wishing to stay, Susan and Peter have a well-equipped cottage to let. With many picturesque walks around The Narth, The Trekkers is an ideal stopping-off point for visitors and locals alike.

The Trekkers, The Narth, nr Trelleck 0600 860367 Map Ref: 4G

The Crown at Whitebrook is reached on from the B4293 where a signpost one and a half miles before Trelleck, takes you into the Whitebrook Valley where you will find the Crown two miles down a narrow country lane, on the right.

The Crown at Whitebrook, nr Trelleck 0600 860254 Map Ref: 4G

The proprietors, Sandra and Roger Bates say it is described as a 'restaurant with rooms', mainly because it specialises in food with a French flavour. The chef prepares everything freshly, and the menu is a culinary delight. However, the twelve ensuite,attractively furnished bedrooms are equally as special as the food. The situation of The Crown is lovely, tucked away in the Whitebrook Valley, close enough to the Brecon Beacons National Park and the forest of Dean: a marvellous area for those who love to walk.

On route to Monmouth we passed through **Mitchel Troy** and discovered **Church Farm Guest House** in this quiet village, opposite the Norman church and the charming home of Derek and Rosemary Ringer who also run Wysk Walks, a business which provides walking weeks and short break holidays within the surrounding countryside. A 16th century former farmhouse, Church Farm features magnificent timbered ceilings and inglenook fireplaces and is tastefully furnished throughout. Accommodation is provided for non-smokers in eight attractive and well-equipped bedrooms, most are en-suite and all meals can be provided. Outside in the acre of woodland gardens with stream you can see many varieties of birds, whilst in an outbuilding, Rosemary has a small pottery where you may be able to purchase samples of her work including vases, jugs and tableware.

Church Farm Guest House, Mitchel Troy 0600 712176 Map Ref: 3G

Having thoroughly explored the splendid Wye Valley and its surroundings, we arrived at the prosperous market town of **Monmouth**. The town is an excellent touring base for the Wye Valley and has many good hotels. Charles I is alleged to have stayed at the King's Head although it is unlikely that it had that name then! Monmouth Castle was the birthplace of Henry V in 1387. A statue in Agincourt Square commemorates this historic link and reminds us of

19

Monmouth, Monnow Bridge.

the king's famous victory at the Battle of Agincourt in 1415. Another interesting place is the 14th century St Mary's Church. Its belfry has eight bells allegedly recast from a peal Henry V bought back from France. The story goes that as Henry was leaving Calais the ringing of bells was heard and he was told that the French were celebrating his departure. He immediately turned back and liberated the bells for presentation to his native town. Another famous son is Geoffrey of Monmouth, Prior of St Mary's and later bishop of the cathedral of St Asaph in North Wales. It was probably in Monmouth that Geoffrey wrote his massive work, 'A History of the Kings of Britain', with its legends of Merlin and Arthur. Look out for the elaborately carved Geoffrey's Window in the building (now a Youth Hostel) along the street leading northwards from Agincourt Square.

Three rivers meet at Monmouth, the Wye, Monnow and Trothy, all noted for their fishing. The Wye is crossed by a five arched bridge built in 1617. The Monnow, though, boasts the most noteworthy bridge. The three arched Monnow Bridge has a sturdy fortified gatehouse, the only one of its kind in Britain, which dates from medieval times. From our experience in driving through it, the narrow, defended entrance still serves something of its original purpose, for modern traffic has the greatest difficulty in negotiating this ancient obstacle.

In the town's Glendower Street is the Monmouth Museum with its exceptional collection of items relating to Admiral Lord Nelson. His connection with the town was slight but the memorabilia was donated by Lady Llangattock, mother of Charles Stuart Rolls, pioneer airman, motorist and co - founder of Rolls Royce. Rolls's statue is in front of the Shire Hall in Agincourt Square. The museum has the very telescope which Nelson raised to his blind eye at Copenhagen. The Naval Temple, opened in the early 19th century to commemorate Britain's victories at sea, stands on the hill known as The Kymin overlooking the town. The views from the top of this 840ft high hill looking across the Wye and Monnow Valleys are marvellous. In the 18th century, a group of men known as the Kymin Club met here once a week, and in 1794 built their own pavilion, the Round House. This was followed by the Naval Temple, which is decorated with plaques commemorating 15 admirals and their most famous battles. We were glad to hear that this impressive spot will remain just as it is, thanks to the fact that it is in the safe hands of the National Trust.

A stone's throw from the historic Monnow Bridge and with views of the famous Kymin, **The Riverside Hotel** is the ideal base for travellers to Wales. All 17 bedrooms are en-suite including the family room which can accommodate three children and a baby. Delicately decorated, the rooms have recently been renovated and include tea

21

and coffee making facilities. Rodney and Judith Dodd work hard at providing personal service for their guests but if they own the bricks and mortar of The Riverside Hotel, the attractive Long Bar with its cosy Chesterfield settees, belongs to the people of Monmouth. Any night of the week you can find the local postman and his son, the builder, fire chief, plasterers and painters and, of course, Dave. He sits on one of the custom-made bar stools at the end of the bar with his personalised beer glass, and if there is anything you need to know about Monmouth or the surrounding area, Dave can tell you. The Riverside Restaurant is run by chef Neil Johns. The atmosphere is created by brass coach lamps and flickering candlelight. The pink button-backed chairs ensure comfort but it's the delicious cuisine that will keep you lingering at your table. Salmon from the neighbouring River Wye infused with fresh mint and served with a raspberry hollandaise is chef Neil's favourite recipe as the fish is top quality and so very fresh. He asks his customers to be patient as he adds his own personal touches to each dish, but good food is always worth waiting for. Fresh apricots lightly poached and served with a marsala sabayan sauce are a sweet finale to a different dining experience.

The Riverside Hotel, Monmouth 0600 715577/713236 Map Ref: 3G

From commis cook at Gleneagles in Scotland to Executive Manager of 600-bedroom hotels in South East Asia, Rodney Dodd's experience alone makes him more than qualified to provide the standard of service required by today's traveller. Although his wife Judith has no formal training, her artistic flair and dedication to the public through her years as a professional dancer in the Royal Ballet Company stand her in good stead behind the bar. The Riverside Hotel has style and personality but most importantly, it is a friendly hotel.

North west, towards the Black Mountains but close to the many amenities both rural and urban we would reccomend for first class self-catering accommodation, you seek out **Steppes Farm Cottages**, which enjoy a delightful, rural location on the outskirts of **Rockfield** village, just 10 minutes drive from Monmouth. Sleeping between three and six, these charming cottages have been converted from former farm outbuildings parts of which date back to the 14th century. Each one is individually furnished to a very high standard and provides every modern convenience, whilst retaining many original features such as large open fireplaces and exposed oak beams.

Steppes Farm Cottages. Rockfield, Monmouth 0600 71 6273 Map Ref: 3G

Set in such beautiful and tranquil surroundings and yet within easy reach of the historic town of Monmouth and other local places of interest, it is hard to imagine a nicer holiday base.

After Monmouth we decided to head for **Usk** along the **A40**, a scenic road designated as holiday route by the powers that be. Before our next intended stop at **Raglan,** we must mention a campers and caravanners ideal holiday and touring base at **The Bridge Caravan and Camping Site** which is signposted off the **A449** at the Abergavenny/Raglan junction.

An extremely well-equipped site, it carries a five - tick rating from the Welsh Tourist Board for its facilities. These include a modern shower/toilet block, a laundry room with washing machine and tumble dryer and a separate dishwashing room, ensuring you have everything you need for a relaxing holiday.

The Bridge Caravan Park & Camping Site, Dingestow 0600 83241 Map Ref: 3G

We are especially interested in castles and, having seen the first stone castle in Britain at Chepstow, were keen to see a fortress that represented the final phase of castlebuilding. **Raglan Castle,** just off the A40 you can see it from the road has a handsome, decorative appearance. This castle may look less purposeful than some of

Wales's earlier, more robust fortresses. Nevertheless, it must have been strong enough, for it endured the longest seige of the Civil War from June to August 1646. It was built in the more settled later Middle Ages of the 15th and 16th centuries, when greater consideration could be given to decoration and home comforts. Raglan's most outstanding feature is its Great Tower, which stands surrounded by a waterfilled moat separate from the rest of the castle.

Did You Know...

There is a full

Town and Village Index

at the back of the book?

Two miles from Raglan in the hilltop hamlet of **Kingcoed**, you'll find **Moatenwell** a lovely Victorian house on the ridge facing south, set in delightful grounds. The accommodation is excellent, a self-contained wing of the house, comprising an en-suite twin bedroom on the first floor and sitting/dining room below. The wing has a key of its own so you can come and go as you please.

Moatenwell, Kingcoed, Near Raglan 0291 690172 Map Ref: 4F

Now, we turned south along the A449 for **Usk**, a delightful small town set on the banks of the river from which it takes its name. Like Monmouth, it too has the remains of a castle (in private ownership) and a fine square. Fishing is excellent locally. The Usk is a fine salmon fishing river, attracting angling enthusiasts from far and wide. The Gwent Rural Life Museum in New Market Street has display of the county's rural past since 1800 including wagons, craft tools and

Raglan Castle.

vintage machinery. All of these are housed in a renovated 17th century barn which has an adjacent Victorian cottage. We liked Usk a lot. The neat little town is proud of its appearance, and makes special efforts to add colour to its streets with attractive floral displays in summer.

Glen-yr-Afon House Hotel in this lovely market town is a luxurious base from which to tour this beautiful area of South Wales. Enjoying a secluded setting in three acres of lawned gardens with the river Usk running alongside, it is ideal for that 'spoil yourself' break. The public rooms and bars are beautifully furnished and have a relaxed, comfortable air, as does the library, a unique octagonal room topped by a spire, which makes an unusual conference venue as well as providing somewhere for guests to sit and read. There are 26 well-equipped guest rooms all with en-suite facilities and two comfortable lounges to relax in, whilst the oak-panelled dining room provides a lovely setting in which to savour the excellent homecooked cuisine.

Glen-Yr-Afon House, Usk 0291 672302 Map Ref: 5E

The oldest inn in Usk is **The Cross Keys** on Bridge Street, dating back to about 1350. The interior confirms this, a delightful copper topped bar, low ceilings and original stone walls.

The oak fireplace is original and the old oak staircase and ceiling are listed. Because it lies so low by the river, the pub has suffered constantly from flooding over the years, the last time being 1979 but since then a flood prevention wall has been built. The pub has excellent guest beers which are traditional and come from different breweries and are regularly alternated. At The Cross Keys you can choose to eat the bar food with its constant change of daily specials or in the restaurant Children are very welcome in the patio garden at the rear of the pub and inside when they eat.

Cross Keys, Usk 02913 2535 Map Ref: 5E

From Usk we left the main roads for a while and headed in a north westerly direction to once again explore the peaceful countryside. This is truly lovely country and visitors to the Wye Valley will find a peaceful haven for non-smokers at **Ty-Gwyn**, situated just two miles from the picturesque town of Usk. A working cattle and horse farm, with magnificent views of Brecon Beacons National Park (within six miles). Jean Arnett is your charming hostess who has been welcoming guests for many years and will spoil you with her excellent culinary skills. There are three spacious and attractively furnished en-suite guest rooms and you can relax in the comfort of the conservatory which overlooks the lawned garden. The hearty homecooked breakfast has the added attraction of free-range eggs and homemade preserves and sets you up perfectly for a day exploring and sightseeing. Vegetarians and own wine welcome. Sorry no pets or children.

Ty-Gwyn Farm, Gwehelog, Usk 0291 672878 Map Ref: 5E

Returning to the **A449,** we drove southwards away from Gwent's rolling borderlands. But before we left them completely, we stopped place whose unusual name caught our eye. We wondered why anyone would want to call such a fresh, clean looking building **The Rat Trap**. For that is the name of an excellent Hotel and restaurant which lies adjacent to the A449 on the road running from Usk to Chepstow. Apparently for years it was a pub and acquired the name from the local farmers who were the base of the local trade. As one of them explained to us, "It was an escape hole from the missus". Much has changed since those years. Five years ago it was redeveloped and is now suitably modern but not so much that it becomes an eyesore in very beautiful countryside. There is a golden look about it with nice dark contrasting paintwork and stone flower pots decorating low walls surrounding the vast car park.

All the accommodation is centrally heated with shower or bathroom/wc en-suite, coloured television, telephone and tea and coffee making facilities in well decorated rooms.

In the Rat Trap restaurant we found a full menu of freshly prepared food supported by a wine list. There are carefully selected vintages from the major wine producing countries of the world. In addition the Rat Trap house wines are very popular and certainly excellent value for money. If you do not want to eat in the restaurant and would prefer a bar meal then a special menu is produced which can be eaten in the bar at midday and in the evening. Someone was having a wedding reception while we were there and they were specially catered for in the restaurant which was delightfully decorated and full of flowers. We understand they cater for all sorts of private functions and receptions. A very; useful place to go, with its excellent service and of course ample parking space.

The Rat Trap, Llangview, Near Usk 0291 673288 Map Ref: 5E

Sporting facilities are readily available locally. You can try your hand at gliding, fishing, wind surfing, grass skiing, hunting and golfing. If you would rather seek out the area's marvellous history, you will have a wonderful time. Tintern Abbey, Caerleon, the birthplace of Arthur's Merlin, Chepstow and Raglan Castles are close by. The whole area of the Wye Valley is gorgeous and The Rat Trap makes it so easy for you to enjoy a holiday.

In the Parish of **Llantrissant,** two and a half miles south of Usk, you can discover the delights of a superb watering-hole. **The Greyhound Inn/Hotel,** a six hundred year old Welsh longhouse with stone barns, large gardens and car park, is truly a very traditional country inn. Six Real Ales, extensive wines and superb home cooking are served in any of the five cosy rooms. Snuggle by the log fires in Winter or eat outside in the mature gardens in Summer. The converted stone stables offer ten fully furnished country rooms, all en-suite, which have been awarded four Crowns by the Welsh Tourist Board. Stroll across the car park and you can shop for antique and country pine furniture in another of the barns. With all these facilities and the beautiful surrounding countryside of the Usk Valley, a stay at The Greyhound is one you will remember with pleasure.

The Greyhound Inn, Llantrissant 0291 672505/673447 Map Ref: 5E

Another place we would reccomend in the centre this charming village is **The Royal Oak**, a superb combination of friendly local pub, top class hotel and excellent restaurant. Welcoming host Tim Gascoine has successfully retained all the original charm of this delightful 15th century building, whilst at the same time providing every modern amenity.

The traditional oak-beamed bar serves a selection of fine real ales in addition to a wide range of wines, spirits and liqueurs. By contrast, the restaurant has a country garden feel with pretty floral furnishings enhancing a relaxing setting in which you can savour an extensive and mouthwatering menu. Finally, to bed. The twenty-two en-suite guest rooms are all furnished and equipped to the highest standard, some with four-poster bed, and each ensuring a restful and refreshing night's sleep.

The Royal Oak, Llantrissant 0291 673317 Map Ref: 5E

Self-catering enthusiasts will soon realise that, as its name suggests, **Wentwood Forest Retreat** is precisely that. Comprising two self-contained flats, the accommodation is situated within a 20 acre rare-breed smallholding, home to Walt and Anne Jackson. Always open, the smallholding has glorious views over the Brecon Beacons, and direct access to Wentwood Forest and the Usk Valley Walk. **The Retreat** (WTB Self Catering Grade 5), sleeping up to six, is equipped to a very high standard and has an open fire and garden. **The Dairy**, at the opposite end of the 20 acres, sleeps up to four and has a patio. Both flats have a colour TV, fridge-freezer, washing machine and their own mountain views. Children and dogs are welcome. Anne, a published writer, is glad to arrange creative writing tuition with visitors.

Wentwood Forest Retreat, Little Wentwood Farm, Llantrisant
0291 673797 Map Ref: 5E

Penhow Castle.

For those in search of quiet luxury, **Cwrt Bleddyn Hotel** near Usk is ideal. Off the **A449** travelling through **Usk,** turn left after the stone bridge and continue towards **Caerleon** for four miles where you will discover this idyllic haven. Dating back to the 14th century, Cwrt Bleddyn has been tastefully modernised over the years to successfully blend the finest facilities with a traditional country house atmosphere. The Country Club offers a comprehensive range of leisure activities, whilst the hotel itself provides sumptuous accommodation in 25 guest rooms and eleven suites. With superb cuisine served in the elegant Nicholls Restaurant and the use of the Oak Room for private dinner parties, you will find yourself not wanting to leave this corner of heaven!

Cwrt Bleddyn Hotel, Tredunnock, Near Usk 063349 521 Map Ref: 5E

On reaching the outskirts of **Newport,** we took the **A48** to **Penhow**, where there is a fascinating historic site which claims to be Wales's oldest lived in castle. For us, the visit was made all the more interesting because it was conducted by personal stereo Walkman system, a self guided tour with headset which tells you everything about the castle's 850 year history. Penhow's 15th century Great Hall, complete with minstrels' gallery, was particularly impressive.

There is so much history on display in this fascinating border region. We had already seen plenty of evidence, in the shape of castles, of the warlike medieval period when Norman forces swept into Wales, building strongholds as they went. But a similar thing had happened 1,000 years earlier when the Romans marched into these parts. At **Caerleon,** just north of Newport, they established a major garrison town called Isca . Until we visited Caerleon, we had no idea of the wealth of Roman remains here. Along with Chester and York, Caerleon was one of the Romans' most important military bases in Britain. The elite of the Roman army were based here, in what became a large Roman town. For entertainment, the soldiers had a 6,000 seat

Carleon Roman Ampitheatre.

amphitheatre and a huge bathhouse complex (the Roman equivalent to the leisure centres of today). What really surprised us about Caerleon was the extent of the remains. The amphitheatre is still there, and the fortress baths have been excavated and are open to the public. There is also an excellent Legionary Museum where many finds are displayed.

On Penthir Road, on the outskirts of Caerleon, is the **Roman Lodge Hotel.** Beautifully decorated, the hotel's Four Crown accommodation offers you complete relaxation in a warm and friendly atmosphere. Its fifteen well-appointed bedrooms are all en-suite, boasting satellite TV, direct-dial telephone and tea/coffee making facilities as standard. Run by experienced hosts, Brian and Judith Ansen, the hotel has three bars and an à la carte restaurant enjoying a high reputation for food. With José, the Spanish chef in charge, the menu is varied and offers a splendid range of international cuisine. The hotel provides a variety of entertainment, including from Monday to Friday, a resident pianist and, on Saturday nights, a weekly dinner dance.

Roman Lodge Hotel Caerleon 0633 420534/430132 Map Ref: 6E

Wales's third largest conurbation after **Cardiff** and **Swansea** is **Newport** and while the town centre is much like any other, with the usual selection of shops and stores we did find one gem the **Newport Museum and Art Gallery.** (0633 840064) The well presented and imaginatively displayed exhibits cover a wide range of themes including the substantial Roman influence in this part of Wales, represented by an exquisite Roman mosaic floor depicting the four seasons. The town's industrial and maritime history is also recalled here, together with its strong links with the Chartist Movement of the 19th century which campaigned for electoral reform. If you have the time, it's also worth taking a look at Newport's **St Woolos Cathedral,** which crowns a prominent hill above the shopping streets. It stands on a site which has seen religious worship since the 6th century, and has, at its entrance, an ancient little chapel.

One of the most significant late 17th century houses in the whole of the British Isles and just two miles west of Newport town centre is **Tredegar House and Park**, for five hundred years the home of one of the greatest Welsh families, the Morgans, who later became Lords of Tredegar. However, in 1974, the house, together with ninety acres of parkland, became the property of Newport Borough Council. Over the past ten years, tremendous progress has been made, and with the continuing financial support of CADW, Welsh Historic Monuments, the Wales Tourist Board, the Countryside Commission, the Council of Museum in Wales, the Friends of Tredegar House and many others, Newport Borough Council is steadily fulfilling its aim to restore not only the house but also the home farm, stables, gardens and park to something like their original appearance.

Tredegar House, Newport 0633 815880 Map Ref: 6D

For instance the Gilt Room, described in the 1688 inventory as 'the gilted Roome', the decoration is so rich as to make it stand apart in one's memory from the remaining rooms in the house. The Best Chamber, which is located directly above the Gilt Room, was designed only for the use of distinguished guests This room has been recently restored and redecorated and is being furnished as the best of the late seventeenth century bedchambers. In 1982 the Regency fire grate was removed and the eighteenth century Dutch tiles, illustrating the skills of horsemanship, restored and returned to their original location.

Outside the gardens are another delight. They are magically brought to life by the newly acquired 'stereo walkman' tours which take you back in time, around not only the gardens but also the stables and orangery where you'll see the longest shovelboard in the world. The Park at Tredegar ranks as one of the foremost designed landscapes in Wales. Like the house, it has been developed over hundreds of years by successive generations of Morgans and elements from every period of its history can still be traced today.

An excursion towards the coast bought us to **West Usk Lighthouse,** anchored between sea and sky at the mouth of the River Usk. The first of many lighthouses built for Trinity House by James Walker in 1821, its design is unique to the British Isles; a large white circular building with the rooms arranged on two floors in the shape of wedges of cheese, probably the most apt way to describe it, topped by a circular tower which used to house the light room.

West Usk Lighthouse, Wentloog 0633 810126 Map Ref: 5D

Frank and Danielle Sheahan are exceptional hosts of this Guest House accommodation which is available throughout the year. The six bedrooms, most en-suite and all with tea/coffee making facilities, colour TV with piped video and satellite channels, are large, light and airy. The dining room has a distinct maritime feel and you can relax in the guest lounge by the log fire. The unique shape gives rise to several fascinating features, like the solid staircase from the slate bedded hall to the first floor and the ingenious 'well' beneath it, from which water was drawn. The roof garden around the walkround makes sunbathing a delight in the summer. The piece de resistance, is the flotation room, sited on the sea wall with extensive views of the Bristol Channel, you can floated away the stresses of the day.

West Usk offers endless possibilities, guaranteeing that even the most discerning of holiday makers have an enjoyable stay. To name but a few, there is horse riding along the picturesque shoreline, a haven for birdwatchers, as many rare birds have been spotted in the vicinity, and walks along the secluded coastline to the Lighthouse Inn and into the surrounding hills gave us much enjoyment. Golf courses abound and the fishing is excellent.

On **A4042** north from Newport we stopped at **Cwmbran** and recommend **The Parkway Hotel,** a privately owned four star luxury hotel, with seventy en-suite bedrooms all enjoying outstanding views over the surrounding Welsh countryside. Each room is superbly equipped with private bathroom, colour television, radio, direct dial telephone and tea and coffee making facilities. The hotel also recognises the needs of the disabled with specially adapted bedrooms and public areas on the ground floor level with doors to allow wheelchair access. The hotel boasts excellent conference facilities and a health and leisure complex complete with swimming pool, spa bath, sauna, steam rooms, solariums and gymnasium. The Parkway is renowned for the warmth of its welcome, friendly staff and professional service and carries the Wales Tourist Board 5-Crown award.

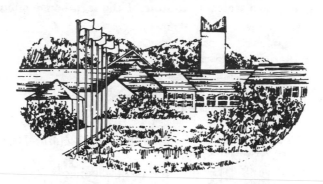

Parkway Hotel & Conference Centre, Cwmbran 0633 871199 Map Ref: 5D

The A4042 leads up into an area of Gwent that is very different from the pastoral greenery of the border country. The old industrial valleys of South Wales, once dominated by the coal, iron and steel industries, are spread across the northern parts of the Gwent and Glamorgan counties. If you are expecting to see coalmines and the ugly scars of industry, then you are in for a pleasant surprise. We were certainly surprised by what we found. The mines have disappeared, forests have been planted, and major environmental improvement schemes have taken away the old eyesores.

Pontypool, the first valleys town we visited, prides itself on being the earliest place in Britain successfully to produce tin plate. That was in 1720 and today the town's industrial past is celebrated at the **Valley Inheritance Centre** in Pontypool Park. At **Llandegfedd Reservoir,** just a few miles from Pontypool, all thoughts of industry seem totally misplaced. Llandegfedd is a popular recreation area with the local folk. Here you can picnic, walk and enjoy the views. Visitors can buy permits for trout and sailing is allowed on the lake. Nature lovers will enjoy birdwatching especially in the winter months when the area is a haunt for wildfowl.

Enjoying a picturesque hillside setting, overlooking the village of **Little Mill, Pentwyn Farm** offers a choice of accommodation that is just that little bit special. Pentwyn is a superb example of a Welsh longhouse, surrounded by beautiful mature gardens complete with swimming pool and boasting outstanding views across the Usk Valley. The house is a picture both inside and out, with lovely period furnishings enhancing a relaxed and welcoming atmosphere. There are four first class en-suite guest rooms and meals here are a delight. There is excellent self-catering accommodation in the converted stables, in the form of two lovely cottages which both sleep four and carry the Welsh Tourist Board Highly Commended rating. Self-catering guests are welcome to dine at the farmhouse should they wish.

Pentwyn Farm, Little Mill, Pontypool 049528 249 Map Ref: 5D

Slightly north you'll find the tiny hamlet of **Mamhilad**, there we discovered that few bed and breakfast farms match **Ty'r Ywen** for comfort or setting. Lying near the crest of Garn Wen Mountain in Brecon Beacons National Park, it commands fine views down the Usk Valley. A sixteenth century Welsh longhouse retaining many original features, the house has been imaginatively converted by hostess Susan Armitage, with all the rooms outstandingly furnished. The four centrally heated bedrooms are en-suite with colour TV and radio. The large lounge and kitchen/dining room have original oak beams. The ancient farmland round about is a walkers' and birdwatchers' paradise. Renowned for its hospitality and superb accommodation, you are assured of a warm welcome at Ty'r Ywen Farm and a place by the inglenook fire.

Ty'r Ywen Farm, Mamhilad, Pontypool Tel/Fax: 0495 785200 Map Ref: 5D

One of Gwent's many former collieries does survive, though its livelihood now comes from visitors, not coal. We spent a few eye opening hours at the **Big Pit Mining Museum, Blaenafon**. Big Pit gives its visitors an authentic insight into South Wales's industrial past, for the pit was a working colliery before becoming a museum of the mining industry. Visitors, accompanied by guides who are ex - miners, descend 300ft underground with safety helmets and cap lamps to experience for themselves the working life of generations of Welsh miners. There's also plenty to see on the surface, including workshops, an engine house, pithead baths and an exhibition of mining techniques. South Wales's metal producing past is also remembered at Blaenafon, for just across the valley from Big Pit there's the Blaenafon Ironworks, an early industrial site which has been preserved and is open to the public.

We travelled on from Blaenafon along a most spectacular mountain road with wonderful views, which dropped down steeply into **Govilon** in the Usk Valley. Govilon's next door neighbour, just about four miles west of **Abergavenny** is the pretty village of **Gilwern**. Here we discovered an ideal place, **The Road House** at the top of the village, where the opportunity to spend a comfortable and peaceful stay amongst good scenery with the chance to enjoy many country pursuits without the need of a car seemed too good to miss. Here John Smith and his wife run a small fleet of three narrowboats on the adjoining **Monmouthshire and Brecon Canal**. The boats are fully equipped for a comfortable weeks cruise for up to six persons and have on board full facilities for cooking, sleeping, a shower, fridge, modern toilet and even a hair drier! John told us that the boats are very easy to handle, and that they are happy to give any assistance you might need during your holiday, particularly if the experience is new to you. The Monmouthshire and Brecon Canal runs south to Pontypool and north-west to Brecon. It lies within the often spectacular scenery of the Brecon Beacons National Park, which is especially beautiful in Spring or Autumn. The boats have central heating so you can be really cosy if the weather turns cool.

There is much to see and do in the area surrounding Gilwern and the canal. If you are energetic, the sky really is the limit. Hang-gliding in this area is breathtaking. Hill walking and pony trekking are very popular which is not surprising when one considers the natural beauty of the National Park. Alternatively, for the less energetic visitor in search peace and tranquillity, Gilwern is an excellent base from which to explore the scenery, with many places of varied interest to suit the whole family. Both families and couples are welcome. Local people are very friendly and helpful, and the village has plenty of shops from which to buy your provisions. There is even a fish and chip shop for a traditional take-away meal.

The Road House, Gilwern 0873 830240 Map Ref: 3C

We also discovered **Maes-y-Berllan**, the charming 18th century farmhouse home of Alan and Myra Lewis who offer first class self-catering accommodation in a beautiful and tranquil location within the Brecon Beacons National Park. The name when translated means "farm in the orchards" and Maes-y-Berllan was the original Welsh longhouse which stood at the heart of the old orchard grounds. With Abergavenny just ten minutes drive away and the famous 'Sugar Loaf Mountain' lying behind, this is a super holiday base, whatever your needs. Within the farmhouse, all the rooms are fully equipped and attractively furnished providing very comfortable accommodation in a homely and relaxed atmosphere. Outside you can stroll through lovely orchards, gardens, or follow the meandering path of the River Usk which borders the farm.

Maes-y-Berllan, Gilwern 0873 830492 Map Ref: 3C

The market town of **Abergavenny,** our next stop, is right on the edge of the Brecon Beacons National Park, 519 square miles of unspoilt moorlands and mountains which contains the highest peaks in South Wales. The park is popular with hikers and climbers as well as less hardy outdoor types like us who simply enjoy being amongst fresh, green countryside. Abergavenny is a well located touring centre for the park, and welcomes many visitors in the summer months. It didn't always have such an hospitable reputation. A chilling story of old Abergavenny relates how in 1176, the Norman knight William de Braose invited the Welsh lords to dine at his castle and then murdered the lot whilst they were disarmed at table! Today the castle offers a more cordial welcome. Its museum has a fascinating collection of old prints, a Welsh kitchen and a saddlery. Try to visit Abergavenny on a Tuesday. Although you'll have difficulty finding a car parking space, the effort will be well worth it for this is the day of the week when the market is held. Farmers with their sheep and cattle come to town and stallholders set up shop in the open air, creating a lively atmosphere.

Clam's Coffee House, Abergavenny 0873 854496 Map Ref: 3D

Renowned for their 'Cakes of Excellence', a visit to **Clam's Coffee House** on King Street, Abergavenny is surely a must. This is a coffee house of the highest order, as is shown by the fact that Clam's supply various tearooms, restaurants, patisseries and coffee shops throughout Wales with their cakes. In prettily decorated surroundings you can sip your tea or coffee from quaint china cups and linger over one of the many mouthwatering temptations on the menu. A licensed establishment, Clam's caters for every meal, with a selection of breakfast dishes as well as various snacks, hot lunches and suppers. Opening times are 9.30am-5.30pm Monday to Wednesday, 9.30am-8.30pm Thursday and Friday, 9.30am-7.00pm on Saturday, and Sunday 10.30am-6.30pm.

Did You Know...

There is a full list of

Tourist Information Centres

at the back of the book?

A couple of miles from Abergavenny, **New Court Farm,** the charming home of Bryan and Janet Nicholls, is a place where you will find excellent bed and breakfast accommodation in a warm, lively atmosphere. Situated on the slopes of **Skerrid Mountain** overlooking Abergavenny, New Court was originally built in 1643 for a local landowner and is a house full of light and spaciousness, lovingly restored by Janet and Bryan with period furnishings adding to its charm. There are four lovely en-suite guest rooms providing all the facilities you would expect, whilst for those who prefer, the Nicholls also have self-catering accommodation available in holiday flats. Outside there is an orchard garden with surrounding views that are simply breathtaking and guests can enjoy many picturesque walks close to the farm.

New Court Farm, Llantilio Pertholey, Abergavenny 0873 852300 Map Ref: 3D

The delightful countryside surrounding Abergavenny has numerous hidden places offering the most relaxing holiday one could wish. The following are our recommendations from our visit to this delightful area. On the edge of **Nant-y-Derry** situated in a lovely spot overlooking the Usk Valley, **Heathfield** is a charming Victorian country guest house owned by Mary Pritchard, which carries a Two - crown Commended rating from the Welsh Tourist Board. Heathfield stands in over an acre of mature gardens complete with patio and barbecue, which command magnificent views all around. This spacious, beautifully furnished house has a relaxed and friendly air and has three lovely guest rooms, one en-suite, but no smoking in the bedrooms please. Mary will happily advise guests of the best walks and places to visit and as she is an experienced cook, you are assured of excellent meals throughout your stay.

Heathfield, Nant-y-Derry, Abergavenny 0873 880675 Map Ref: 3D

James Farrow was trained at The Dorchester and now runs the famous **Foxhunter Inn** at **Nantyderry**. Situated between the **A4042** and **Chainbridge**, this charming inn was originally opened as refreshment rooms by the local vicar, for travellers on the Great Western Railway. It was renamed The Foxhunter in 1962 by Sir Harry Llewellyn whose horse, Foxhunter, won the Helsinki Olympic Games. Visitors here will find the quality of service and presentation and that of the food, wine and ale, reflect Dorchester standards at country inn prices and popularity makes reservations advisable. The Inn has a national and local following and lunch or dinner at this 'hidden' hostelry should not be missed when touring this delightful part of South Wales.

Foxhunter Inn, Nantyderry, Near Abergavenny 0873 88 Map Ref: 3D

West from Abergavenny it is hard to imagine a more peaceful or relaxing setting than that of **Upper Cwm Farm** in **Brynderi**.

Situated just off the **B4233,** old Abergavenny to Monmouth road, it is the third farm at the top of Brynderi Road and is set in 80 acres of rolling countryside. A wealth of beautiful walks lie literally on your doorstep and provide a haven for a wide variety of animal and birdlife. The two spacious apartments, The Granary and The Coach House each sleep six and are housed within a delightful barn conversion, offering every modern comfort, whilst retaining many original features of the building. For peace and sheer natural beauty, Upper Cwm Farm is very hard to beat and will give you a holiday to remember.

Upper Cwm Farm, Llantilio Crossenny 0873 821236 Map Ref: 3D

Lying seven miles from Abergavenny and a mile from Cross Ash, **Lower Green Farm** is a peaceful haven for lovers of self-catering holidays. Set within this working Welsh sheep farm, you will find two fully equipped cottages, beautifully furnished in traditional country cottage style, which sleep between four and six.

Lower Green Farm, Llanfair Green, Cross Ash 0873 821219 Map Ref: 2F

There are wonderful views of Skirrid and the Black Mountains and the surrounding countryside is home to a wealth of animal and birdlife including badgers and wild ducks. There is a safe corner where children can play, with the added attraction of guinea pigs and a donkey to pat. Walkers will delight when they learn that the famous Three Castle Walk which incorporates **Skenfrith, Grosmont** and **White Castle**, passes through the farm grounds.

After exploring the lovely, lush Usk Valley we turned our attentions to the rugged heart of the **Black Mountains,** having been told of a remote valley north of Abergavenny which ran close to the Wales/ England border. To find it, we drove from Abergavenny along the **A465** Hereford road passing the Skirrid Fawr mountain on the right to turn left for **Cwmyoy** and the **Llanthony Valley.**

Grange Trekking Centre, Capel -y- Ffin 0873 890215 Map Ref: 1D

On our way we passed the **Grange Trekking Centre** where, at this family concern you can choose from an hour to whole days riding. Approved by the Pony Trekking and Riding Society of Wales, the centres experienced leaders ensure the visit of riders of all abilities to be a memorable one as you to ride through some beautiful countryside with exhilarating views in the Black Mountains.

Before entering the valley however, we decided to visit **Pandy.** There we found two places that should satisfy all the visitor might need. Set within four acres of farmland just off the main Hereford to Abergavenny road in Pandy, you will find a number of reasons to call in at **Pandy Craft Shop and Tea Room.** The Tea Room also serves as the village Post Office and in addition to enjoying fine homecooked refreshments, you can choose from a delightful display of soft toys which are made on the premises.

Pandy Craft Shop and Tea Rooms, Pandy 0873 890235 Map Ref: 2E

The original tram way runs through the grounds and there is an interesting 71/4 gauge steam engine on display, whilst for guests

Llanthony Priory.

wishing to stay, friendly hostess Mrs. Jean Evans offers very comfortable bed and breakfast accommodation in the main house in three attractively furnished guest rooms. Should you prefer, there are also facilities for campers, ensuring everyone is well-catered for here.

Finally, on the way to **Llanthony** we stopped to look at **Cwmyoy Church**. This really is a strange sight. The church, on the side of a hill, has been the victim of subsidence to such an extent that everything appears to be leaning over on the point of collapse. The tower looked to us as though it was leaning at an angle greater than Pisa's! There is a proliferation of religious sites in this lovely vale. Gerald of Wales, the monk who wrote of his medieval travels around Wales, described Llanthony as a place truly calculated for religion and more adapted to the canonical discipline than all the monasteries of the British Isles. He was referring to Llanthony Priory, which was built on a spot which has links with the earliest glimmerings of Christianity in Wales. During the Age of Saints in the 6th century, Llanthony was chosen by David, Wales's patron saint, for a cell. In the 11th century the Norman warlord William de Lacy found it and was so struck by its peace and sanctity that he built a hermitage which later became the Priory of Llanthony it remains may still be seen. Finally Father Ignatius tried to establish another religious house further up the valley but the project came to nought early this century. The valley's beauty also brought the poet Walter Savage Landor and the designer Eric Gill to live here. For walkers, the Offa's Dyke Path runs along the ridge of wild hills above Llanthony. This off the beaten track location certainly cast a spell over us, influenced, perhaps, by the wonderful accommodation that we found.

Enjoying a dramatic setting two miles from the Offa's Dyke border with England, the magnificent ruins of Augustine Abbey stand proudly, surrounded by the spectacular scenery of the Llanthony Valley. It is here, in part of the original priory that you will discover a simply wonderful holiday retreat, the **Llanthony Abbey Hotel**. Run by Ivor Prentice and his friendly team of staff, this is an enchanting place to stay. Simply furnished in keeping with its monastic background, the guest rooms feature two and four poster beds, some dating to savage landors days and the Crypt Bar and Restaurant provide a unique setting in which to savour such mouthwatering delights as Abbott Casserole or Lamb-de-Lacy, black mountain lamb with mushroom and garlic sauce. This is definitely a place not to be missed.

Llanthony Abbey Hotel, Llanthony 0873 890487 Map Ref: 1D

The Half Moon Inn at Llanthony, is a marvellous place for anyone to stay who is looking for a peaceful holiday in superb countryside. Rob and Chris Minor who run The Half Moon offer activity holiday packages as well which are the great fun for energetic people. They arrange for fly fishing at a local fish farm, and fishing the Honddu river. You are asked to provide your own rod and Welsh Water Rod Licence.

Pony trekking is done from one of the licensed centres in and around the valley. All ages and all sizes are catered for with two full or half day treks depending on how you feel. For clay pigeon enthusiasts the Minors have a sporting shoot consisting of approximately one hundred and sixty birds over two days.

The Half Moon Inn, Llanthony 0873 890611 Map Ref: 1D

The Half Moon itself is a traditional country inn built originally from two 17th century estate cottages on the Llanthony estate, using stone from the ruins of the 11th century Augustinian Priory five minutes walk away. There are nine comfortable bedrooms available for bed and breakfast and they offer set meals by arrangement which cater for any dietary requirement.

Alternatively, lovers of self-catering holidays will find an enchanting holiday base at **Troedrhiwmwn Farmhouse** in Llanthony. Owned by Mary and Gordon Thomas who farm 1000 sheep and beef cattle, this splendid 600 year old Welsh longhouse stands proudly on the hillside offering spectacular views of Llanthony Valley, which is without doubt one of the most beautiful areas in Gwent. The farmhouse is fully equipped to cater for your every need. Logs for the open fire are provided as is the coal for the lovely kitchen Rayburn. Outside there is a barbecue area and ample parking space. Children are allowed to ride the farm pony and feed the farm animals. Fishing for brown trout and grayling is available nearby and on the hillside slopes, if you are lucky, you may discover the Bee Orchid or the Oxeye Cowslip.

Troedrhiwmwn Farmhouse, Llanthony 0873 890619 Map Ref: 1D

Out of the Llanthony Valley just half a mile outside the Black Mountain village of **Fforest, Trewysgoed Riding Centre** provides superb residential and non-residential courses and holidays for riders of all abilities. Sarah Cotton, the owner of this superb establishment is famous as an eventer and trainer/instructor and the centre is B.H.S and A.B.R.S approved so you can be sure the facilities and tuition are of the very highest standard. There are also thirteen very comfortable guest rooms available for those on residential courses. The more experienced rider can take advantage of eventing courses which include dressage, cross country jumping, fittening rides and a competition on the last day. Whatever your needs and abilities, a visit to Trewysgoed Riding Centre is sure to be one to remember.

White Castle.

Trewysgoed Riding Centre, Fforest, nr Abergavenny
0873 890296 / 890855 Map Ref: 3D

To the east of Abergavenny the **Monnow Valley** forms something of a gap in the natural defences of the Welsh Marches between the river cliffs of the Wye Valley and the mountains further west. It was here that Normans built the Three Castles of Gwent - **Skenfrith, White** and **Grosmont.** Skenfrith stands with its church and village beside the Monnow. Built in the 13th century by Hubert de Burgh, it is noted for its fine round tower keep and its well preserved curtain wall. How times have changed along this border. Once, it was the troubled domain of medieval warlords. Today it is peaceful and undisturbed, a perfect area for relaxed, unhurried exploration.

On the **B4521** between **Cross Ash** and **Skenfrith**, you will come to Hop Garden, the home of **Wool, Wheels and Weaving** by a beautiful stream in the soft rolling hills of the Monnow Valley. The studio/shop is an 'Aladdin's Cave' for the fibrecraft enthusiast, novice and experienced alike. There you will find locker-hooking, weaving (including Peg-Loom and Stick-Weaving). Most days one of these crafts is demonstrated. If, having watched a spinning demonstration you feel it is something you would like to do, Frank and Sarah Wuller will let you 'try before you buy' on one of their wide range of spinning wheels. You could purchase a spinning wheel, fibres and any other accessories you need to get started. This is where you can find a Footman - but not too close to the Maidens! Knitters have found their range of studio-dyed natural fibre yarns (mohair, alpaca, silk combinations, etc.) much to their liking. There is also available a small selection of locally produced hand-knitted and woven products. Two books, 'Hooking With Hob-Nob' and 'Stick Weaving', have been written and published by Sarah. Locker-Hooking, a simple canvas

51

craft, is the subject of 'Hooking With Hob-Nob'. 'Stick Weaving' is a very portable method of simple weaving on sticks and is a good introduction to weaving for children and adults alike. Disabled are welcome. Should you be unable to visit the studio/shop and are interested in any of the crafts, call them or write for further details. Their normal business hours are 10.00-5.00 Tuesday to Saturday inclusive. To save disappointment, a phone call first might be best.

Please Don't Forget...

To tell people that you read about them in

The Hidden Places

Wool, Wheels and Weaving. Hop Garden, Skenfrith, Abergavenny 060084 60 Map Ref: 2F

The second of Gwent's Three Castles is **White Castle** near the village of Llanvetherine. It gets its odd name from the time, centuries ago, when its walls were covered with white plaster. That has now gone but other features to note include the fine towers and steep moat which may be crossed by a wooden bridge. Built in about 1180 with additions in the 13th century, the castle had the dubious distinction of being home briefly to Rudolf Hess, Hitler's deputy, who fed the swans in the castle moat.

To complete our look at the famous trio of borderland fortresses we had to take to the country lanes for **Grosmont**. French speakers may have guessed by now that the village's name derives from gros mont ' big hill'. The first castle here was just that a steep earthen mound topped by timber defences, though the stronghold was later rebuilt in stone. An Arabic 'faience jar' found her is a relic of the Crusades. Considering the village's modest size, we were surprised by the magnitude of its church. All was explained by a helpful local, who told us that the church reflected Grosmont's previous importance it was, we discovered to our surprise, a borough up until the mid 19th century.

From Grosmont, we made our way back towards Abergavenny. It was time now to head further west, away from Gwent and into the Glamorgans. The most convenient way was along the A465 which

52

runs across from Abergavenny eventually down to Neath, a route known locally as the **'Heads of the Valleys'** road, as it links all the old industrial valleys of South Wales. The 1992 Garden Festival site in the old steelmaking town of **Ebbw Vale** is certainly worth a visit. Millions of trees, shrubs and flowers have been planted here, and an entire valley environment has been transformed by introducing features such as terraces, gardens, waterfalls and a lake a most impressive achievement, we thought.

Tredegar, a little further along the Heads of the Valleys, was the birthplace of that fiery orator **Aneurin Bevan** who founded our National Health Service. It was in Tredegar too that the novelist **A J Cronin** worked as a doctor and collected the background material for 'The Citadel', later made into a film starring Robert Donat. On the outskirts of Tredegar, there was yet another example of the way in which the old valleys are changing for the better. Bryn Bach Park is a 600 acre stretch of grassland and woodland ranged around the centrepiece of a manmade lake. In its Visitor Centre, we learned that the park has been reclaimed from a derelict and neglected wasteland into a most attractive area where you can fish, walk or enjoy picnics in the open air.

In the nearby hamlet of **Manmoel,** we found our final place to stay as far as this chapter is concerned. However, as that often used saying goes - last but not least we'd reccomend visitors in the area to the warm welcome they'll receive at **Wyrloed Lodge**, the charming home of Norma and Steve James.

Wyrloed Lodge, Manmoel 0495 371198 Map Ref: 2F

This imposing late Victorian farmhouse has been fully refurbished and provides lovely accommodation in three spacious and beautifully co-ordinated guest rooms, each with en-suite facilities and providing every modern comfort. The surrounding two and a half acres of pasture are home to a pedigree flock of Badger Faced Welsh Mountain sheep and there is an abundance of bird and wildlife. There are beautiful walks on all sides and the views from Manmoel mountain are simply breathtaking. With Norma's excellent homecooking to return to each day, a stay at Wyrloed Lodge is one you will remember with pleasure.

We left Gwent contented by the amount of interest this small area had generated for us with its generous sprinkling of history and places of interest. Glamorgan lay before us and as we slipped across the ' border ' we wondered whether we'd be thinking along similar lines when the time came to move further west. The next chapter describes our finds and at the risk of spoiling things, we don't think you'll be disappointed.

CHAPTER TWO

The Glamorgans.

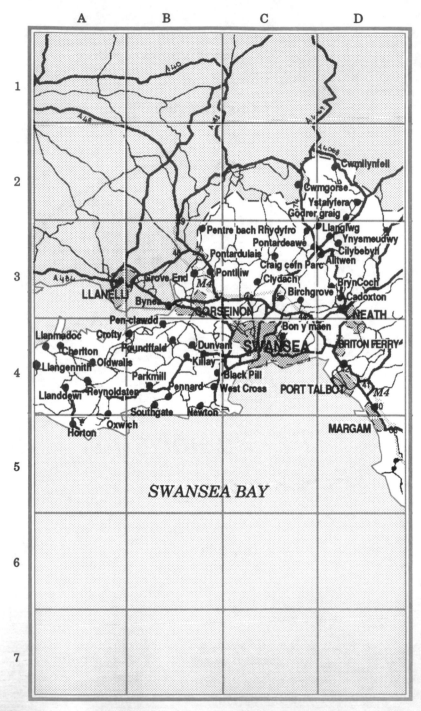

Hengoed Viaduct.

CHAPTER TWO

The Glamorgans.

We were most surprised by what we found in this fascinating part of Wales. Prior to our arrival, we had an image in our minds of an industrial area, of coalmining and grey docklands. These images were as out of date as the films - Tiger Bay and How Green Was My Valley - that largely created them. The valleys, we soon found out, are green again.

Cardiff, Wales's capital city, has some of the most impressive civic architecture we've seen anywhere in our travels. We also found that the old 'industrial' valleys by no means occupy all of this area. The three Glamorgan counties - South, Mid and West - embrace a huge variety of scenery. The **Vale of Glamorgan** in the south is a rich pastoral area of green fields and traditional villages, where you'll even see the occasional thatched cottage. On the northern fringes of the valleys we found spectacular unspoilt uplands, for this countryside borders the **Brecon Beacons National Park.**

The coastline was also spectacular. Glamorgan's cliffs and extensive areas of sand dunes are a protected 'heritage coast', while the lovely **Gower Peninsula** - on the doorstep of **Swansea** (another most attractive city) - was the first part of Britain to be declared an 'Area of Outstanding Natural Beauty'. They say that this part of South Wales is full of surprises - we certainly found more than our fair share during the time we spent here.

The first surprise came along the **A465** 'Heads of the Valleys' road. Driving westwards on this road towards **Merthyr Tydfil**, we noticed the abrupt contrasts between urban and rural that are so much a feature of this part of Wales. The road acts as a dividing line: to our left were the historic valleys once dominated by coalmining and iron-and steel-making, yet to our right were the untouched southern uplands of the Brecon Beacons National Park. This rigidly observed dividing line is explained by geology: The coal-bearing rocks of the valleys end along the line of this road, giving way to the limestone and old red sandstone rocks of the Brecon Beacons.

Geology also explains the growth of industry in these parts. The iron smelting which accompanied the coalmining was a result of the fact that limestone - a key part of the process - was easily quarried locally. Iron ore was also to be found nearby. These ingredients all came together in the most productive way at our first stop, Merthyr Tydfil, the former 'iron and steel capital of the world'.

Cyfarthfa Castle Museum is by no means the only monument in Merthyr to times gone by and is situated in the state rooms of Cyfarthfa Castle, which was built by the Crawshay family of ironmasters in 1825 to overlook their ironworks, then the largest in the world. The family moved out in the 1890s and in 1909 the Borough Council bought the Castle and grounds, principally to use as the town's grammar school. With the support of a group of local collectors and enthusiasts, a museum and art gallery was established, and a professional curator was employed by the Borough until 1920.

There is disabled access into this interesting museum whose bulk of exhibits being collected before 1945 cover many areas amongst which natural history, military history, industrial, social and local history feature.   Since 1986, collecting has been more active, particularly in the field of social history. The building is still shared with a school, and education groups are encouraged to use the museum through contacts with local advisors and the teacher's centre. Merthyr Tydfil is the largest of the South Wales "Valleys" towns, whose fortunes were built on the iron and then coal industries.

Cyfarthfa Castle Museum, Merthyr Tydfil 0685 723112 Map Ref: 3F

Housed, as it is, in what was the opulent home of an all-powerful ironmaster, it inevitably makes us think of the privilege and wealth created by the Industrial Revolution. The other side of the coin - the living conditions of the workers - is also remembered a little way down the road at **Joseph Parry's Cottage.** Parry was a famous 19th-century composer (he wrote the haunting hymn Myfanwy which is a favourite performance piece with male-voice choirs). He was born in a tiny terraced cottage - now renovated and open to the public - almost within the shadow of grand **Cyfarthfa Castle.**

Close by is yet another reminder of Merthyr's former industrial pre-eminence, the **Ynysfach Engine House.** Originally opened in 1801, it was the first furnace to use steam power and was soon producing more iron than furnaces at Cyfarthfa. It suffered as steel production replaced that of iron and by 1879 was closed. It was saved from total ruin by the Merthyr Tydfil Heritage Trust and in 1989 opened as a Heritage Centre for the Iron Industry in the area.

Dowlais, on the hillside above the town centre, was one of Merthyr's busiest districts when the blast furnaces and foundries were turning out metal for world markets as far apart as the Russian Steppes and South America. In the 19th century, the skies were bright day and night with the glow from the ironworks. Dowlais has seen tremendous changes since its industrial heyday.

Whilst visiting Merthyr Tydfil, incidentally the biggest town in Wales, you will find a delightful place to stay at **Tregenna Hotel** which enjoys a peaceful but central location behind the town's Roman Catholic church. This is a lovely family-run establishment with twenty one superbly equipped en-suite guest rooms, and an attractively furnished restaurant and dining area which has a strong local following, popular for its excellent homecooked traditional fayre. Tregenna also provides alternative accommodation in four 4-bedroomed, luxury detached houses as well as several well-equipped holiday cottages, ensuring all guests are well-catered for.

Tregenna Hotel, Merthyr Tydfil 0685 723627 Map Ref: 3F

Merthyr is on the doorstep of lovely countryside - it's literally a five-minute drive from the Brecon Beacons National Park. Just a mile or so from Cyfarthfa Castle is the pretty little village of **Pontsticill**, surrounded by green hills, lakes and forests. **Pengelli Fach Farm and Riding School** at Pontsticill is a small working hill farm which provides super holidays for the rider or the non rider in glorious countryside. There are three guest rooms, all en suite and very comfortably furnished and with the Wales Tourist Boards stamp of approval. There is a separate lounge with colour TV and also a separate dining room.

Riders are provided with a variety of courses which can be virtually tailored to any rider's needs. If you have never ridden before Pengelli is the ideal place to start; you will be taught by sympathetic and mature instructors. You can choose from a number of courses and for the non rider Pengelli is a wonderful place to stay. Surrounded by hill country in and around Pontsticill you can enjoy many country pursuits.

Pengelli is also close to the many attractions and towns in this area of the Glamorgans.

Pengelli Fach Farm and Riding School, Pontsticill Map Ref: 2G

When we were in Pontsticill, we noticed a steam train puffing along the opposite side of the valley. This was the **Brecon Mountain Railway,** which runs on a short but highly scenic line from the northern end of Merthyr Tydfil to a lakeside terminus just beyond Pontsticill. We couldn't resist a ride on this charming narrow-gauge line, which was created with much sweat and toil by enthusiasts of the Age of Steam on the course of an old British Rail route from Merthyr to Brecon. The views from the lakeside terminus, which look out across the waters towards the peak of **Pen-y-fan,** the highest summit in South Wales, are marvellous

Our next stop was at **Aberdare**, a friendly town at the northern end of the Cynon Valley. The valleys are famous for their male-voice choirs - if you ask locally, you can usually sit in on their practice nights. Singing is a strong tradition in South Wales, and musicians are revered. Aberdare is no exception in this respect. It must be the only town in Britain which has for its main monument the statue of a choir conductor, Griffith Rhys Jones (1834-97), baton in hand, conducting the traffic in Victoria Square.

Although Aberdare's roots came from the Industrial Revolution, don't expect to see much evidence of coalmining today. The valleys, as we said earlier, are green again, thanks to ambitious land reclamation and environmental improvement schemes that have transformed the area in the last 20 years or so. We didn't have to look far for evidence of the changing face of the South Wales valleys, for just a stone's throw from Aberdare's busy town centre we came across the **Dare Valley Country Park.** Created on former colliery land this wooded park has trails that inform you of the natural and industrial history of the area.

The valleys of South Wales are renowned for their friendliness. We

Brecon Mountain Railway.

found it easy to strike up conversations in the shops and pubs with the locals, who were more than keen to offer advice on what to visit. One of them told us about the lovely little hamlet of **Llanwonno**, in the forested hills between the Cynon and Rhondda Valleys. A minor mountain road led to this delightful spot, which consists of no more than an old church, pub and row of cottages. It seems a world removed from the tightly packed terraces of the valleys below, yet is only a short drive from the main road.

Llanwonno is associated with the strange legend of **Guto Nyth-Bran,** the 18th-century long-distance runner whose speed became legendary in this part of Wales. According to legend, he ran across the mountain to fetch yeast in the time that it took for his mother to boil a kettle of water. See if you can find Guto's grave (his real name was Gruffydd Morgan) in the churchyard.

Pontypridd is another friendly valleys town. It comes alive especially on Wednesdays and Saturdays, when the streets are packed with stalls and shoppers who come from far and wide for market day. Like Merthyr Tydfil, Pontypridd is proud of its past. An old chapel near Pontypridd's historic stone bridge across the River Taff is the home of the **Pontypridd Historical and Cultural Centre**. In the town's attractive Ynysangharad Park there are two statues commemorating Evan and James James, a father-and-son songwriting team responsible for composing the words and music of the Welsh National Anthem, **Hen Wlad fy Nhadau**. Wales's 'Land of Song' image seems to be at its strongest in these parts. Pontypridd and district has produced an amazing trio of world-famous singers. Opera star Sir Geraint Evans and Stewart Burrows were born - in the same street! - in nearby Clifynydd, while Tom Jones is another local hero.

When we visited the Big Pit Mining Museum at Blaenafon (see Chapter One), we were told of another place - **The Rhondda Heritage Centre** (0443 682036) - dedicated to telling the story of South Wales's coalmining past. Only a handful of pits now survive in the Welsh valleys - in the booming 19th-century there were hundreds - so it's not at all correct, as we soon discovered, to think of modern South Wales in terms of heavy industry. Miners now account for only a tiny percentage of the workforce, yet the strong traditions of the mining valleys are rightly cherished. This was brought home to us vividly at the Rhondda Heritage Centre based at former colliery sites at **Trehafod** on the **A4058** from Pontypridd to Porth. The Heritage Centre is an on-going project which will tell future generations of an industry that shaped South Wales, but is now coming to an end. Machinery and mining equipment are on display, and visitors can see an imaginative 'Black Gold' presentation.

Caerphilly Castle

We decided to head south now, out of the valleys. But before we left this distinctive, welcoming part of Wales altogether, we drove via **Nelson** to **Ystrad Mynach**, where you can see the sixteen arched **Hengoed Viaduct**, built in 1857 to cater for one of the busiest stretches of railway in the area; before taking the **A469** south to Caerphilly and yet another surprising sight. Right in the middle of this otherwise unremarkable town there's a castle of quite incredible proportions. **Caerphilly Castle** is one of Britain's largest castles and amongst the greatest surviving examples of medieval military architecture in Europe. This book is called 'Hidden Places', and there can surely be no site that is more unknown - unjustly so in our opinion - than Caerphilly Castle. Probably the location has a lot to do with Caerphilly's unwarranted obscurity. More and more visitors are now discovering the castle, so you should see it before it becomes overrun with tourists. The castle was built largely in the late 13th century by the Norman lord Gilbert de Clare. He created a mighty 'stone and water' system of concentric defences which can still be seen today, together with a formidable gatehouse rising above the waters of the moat. The castle also has a leaning tower (which manages to out lean Pisa's world famous example!).

It was only a short drive from Caerphilly to **Cardiff**, Wales's capital city and a delightful place. Again we were unprepared for the unexpected beauty and style of the place. Cardiff's Civic Centre is an architectural masterpiece. White stoned buildings of classical design, **The National Museum of Wales** and **City Hall** amongst them, are set in wide, tree lined avenues and green parklands. The overall effect is quite stunning, and it's easy to see why this collection of buildings is regarded as one of the world's most accomplished examples of civic architecture. Close by is **Cardiff Castle**, a unique three in one historic site that began life as a Roman fort, evolved into a medieval castle, and was transformed into a lavish mansion in the 19th century by the Marquess of Bute.

The story of Cardiff is the story of the Bute family. They controlled the docklands, and as Cardiff boomed as a coal exporting port the family made a vast fortune. Some of this wealth was poured into the wholesale reconstruction of Cardiff Castle, an expense - no - object exercise for which the architect and 'eccentric genius' William Burges was employed. Burges's flamboyant imagination was allowed to run riot, the result being a glittering, opulent set of rooms that have to be seen to be believed. The castle also preserves its links with the more distant past, for the gounds contain a well preserved medieval keep and stonework dating from Roman times.

No visit to Cardiff would be complete without paying a visit to **The**

Cardiff.

Welsh Love Spoons, which is situated in the arcade opposite Cardiff's historic castle. Proprietor Mike Davies is recognised as one of the foremost wood carvers in Europe and it is a privilege to watch such skill being applied to the beautiful Welsh fruit wood. The carved love spoon is quintessentially Welsh and the revival of this ancient craft, believed to date back as far as the 16th century, owes much to Mike's work. What finer memento of your visit here, than to purchase one of these exquisitely crafted spoons. Today Mike exhibits and sells his work throughout the world and his customers range from very ordinary folk to the rich and famous, including HRH the Queen Mother and various Heads of State.

The Welsh Love Spoons, Cardiff 0222 231500 Map Ref: 6H

We enjoyed our stay in Cardiff tremendously. There was so much to see, and the shops were most tempting. We were most impressed by the city's mixture of old and new there were, for example, canopied Victorian arcades close to the up to the minute **St David's Shopping Centre** and its marvellous covered market, which has one of the best fresh fish stalls we've seen anywhere.

Situated half way along Cathedral Road in Cardiff within walking distance of the city's historic castle, **Lincoln Hotel** makes a soothing haven for a quiet break and is ideal as a touring base for this lovely area. Formerly two Victorian merchant's houses, this magnificent establishment lies within a conservation area and has been awarded a 4-Crown rating by the Welsh Tourist Board and a 2-Star rating by the AA. The hotel interior is simply stunning with period fabrics and furniture enhancing an air of grand elegance, not least in the charming dining room, where you can savour the finest cuisine accompanied by a carefully selected wine list. The eighteen en-suite guest rooms are furnished to the same high standards, ensuring a refreshing night's rest for all who stay here.

Lincoln Hotel, Cardiff 0222 395558 (Fax: 0222 230537) Map Ref: 6H

In Cardiff, we also walked past that shrine of rugby, the **Arms Park,** where the emotional pre match singing can bring a lump to the throat of the hardiest supporter. This part of Cardiff also has other musical associations, for Ivor Novello, the composer and matinee idol, was born near the grounds. Two of his most memorable songs were 'We'll gather lilacs in the spring' and 'Keep the home fires burning'. A mile or so from the city centre we visited **Llandaff Cathedral,** a beautiful building set in a grassy hollow beside the **River Taff**. The cathedral suffered severe bomb damage during the Second World War. Part of its restoration included a controversial modern sculpture entitled 'Christ in Majesty' by Sir Jacob Epstein, which dominates the interior. This towering, uncompromising piece is still the source of much discussion and comment.

The Angel Hotel, Cardiff 0222 232633 Map Ref: 6H

Overlooking Cardiff Castle and the Arms Park is the oldest hotel in Cardiff, **The Angel Hotel**. Built in 1883, the Angel Hotel is full of history, uniquely positioned between these two ancient and modern landmarks. The fully qualified staff are fully aware of the heritage and traditions of the hotel and aim to make the visitors stay as welcome and relaxed as possible. The Hotel has its own traditional bar, the 'Angel Tavern', a cocktail bar and restaurant. The Hotel also boasts its very own beauty salon and leisure club to make the visitors stay in Cardiff as relaxing and enjoyable as possible.

Tucked away in a quiet backwater just five minute's walk from Llandaff Cathedral, **Plas-y-Bryn** is a delightful 'hidden place' well worth seeking out. Situated on Fairwater Road, this charming Edwardian house stands in attractive gardens and makes a peaceful and relaxing place to stay. Comfortable accommodation is provided in three lovely guest rooms, all beautifully decorated and individually styled with carefully coordinated furnishings. Your welcoming hostess Mari Lougher is an excellent cook and provides an extensive breakfast menu which will set you up well for the day and after exploring the surrounding area you can look forward to a refreshing night's rest here.

Plas-y-Bryn, LLandaff, Cardiff 0222 561717 Map Ref: 6H

Quite close to Llandaff, on the outskirts of the city, is the **Welsh Folk Museum** at **St Fagans**. This was one of the first of the new breed of open air museums that you now come across all over Britain. But the Welsh Folk Museum is something special. Old buildings from all over Wales have been brought here and reconstructed, stone by stone, timber by timber, in a beautiful parkland setting. There are farmhouses, workers' cottages, a toll house, cock pit, mill, tannery and chapel, and regular demonstrations of traditional crafts. Our favourite building was a schoolhouse complete with the old fashioned desks and blackboard.

On our way out from Cardiff we found one 'hidden' gem well worth seeking out, **Llwyn Celyn House** which lies tucked away in peaceful seclusion on a private estate in **Whitchurch** off Pantmawr Road. This large modern house is the charming home of a very friendly lady, Miriam Maugham, who enjoys sharing it with her many guests. Immaculately furnished throughout, very comfortable accommodation is provided in one large, en-suite family room. Miriam is a superb cook and her knowledge of continental and North American dishes gives dining a truly international flavour, with breakfasts ranging from full English to Continental, American and Spanish, and optional evening meals can be provided. With ready access from here to the coast, Cardiff Airport and the Vale of Glamorgan, this Two Crown Commended establishment makes a perfect holiday base.

Llwyn Celyn House, Whitchurch, Cardiff 0222 692685 Map Ref: 6H

We discovered another place enjoying a secluded and somewhat 'hidden' setting on the hillside above the village of **St. Brides-Super-Ely**. **Sant-Y-Nyll** is the splendid country home of Mr. and Mrs. Renwick who welcome guests all year round.

Sant-Y-Nyll, St. Brides-Super-Ely 0446 760209 Map Ref: 6F

71

Set within six acres of woodland and gardens, this magnificent house is truly an oasis of tranquility and beauty, yet lies just fifteen minutes drive from Cardiff. The interior is simply stunning, with beautifully co-ordinated furnishings and country house style furniture enhancing the air of peace and elegance. The six guest rooms are all well-equipped and one has en-suite bathroom. The residential licence means you can enjoy a drink with the excellent three-course dinner provided. Additional accommodation is provided in two lovely self-catering cottages within the grounds.

Did You Know...

The Hidden Places Series
Covers most of Britain?
For our full list see back of book

From the Wales of bygone times we returned to the Wales of today when we joined the M4 motorway westwards. The M4 has brought tremendous benefits to South Wales by improving communications with London and the South East and encouraging new industry into the region. The Japanese have moved into South Wales in a big way, and major manufacturers such as Ford have also large factories here. Another large employer is the Royal Mint at **Llantrissant.**

Built about 160 years as a coaching house where the horses were changed before going up the hill to the historic city of Llantrissant, the capital of Wales in the days of the Black Prince, **The Miskin Arms** is a fine pub with a good local reputation. It is a very cheery pub with a country style bar and has a delightful old world feel about it Weather permitting you can sit outside in the attractive, well - tended gardens. Reasonably priced bar food is available with a menu that should appeal to children. The Miskin Arms also provides bed and breakfast accomodation in six comfortable rooms, two of which are en-suite.

Miskin Arms, Llantrissant 0443 224346 Map Ref: 5F

It's worth taking a trip up the hill into the old town of Llantrissant. We were intrigued by a statue, standing in the Bull Ring, of a figure dressed in a fox skin head dress. One of the locals told us that this was the town's memorial to Dr. William Price, an amazing character who lived from 1800 to 1893. Dr. Price espoused many causes which scandalised straight laced Victorian Britain. He was a vegetarian who believed in free love, nudism and radical politics. His most famous or infamous, at the time deed was his attempt in 1884 to cremate his illegitimate son Iesu Grist (Jesus Christ), who had died in infancy. As a result of the controversy and the ensuing court case, cremation became legal in Britain. To the south of Llantrissant lies the lovely Vale of Glamorgan.

Into **Cowbridge**, a handsome, prosperous town with a historic status as the 'capital of the Vale of Glamorgan'. The town is entered around its long main street, where we found a most appealing selection of shops selling everything from local crafts to books.

Cowbridge has been a busy meeting place for many centuries it has been a market town for almost 1,000 years and is surrounded by historic sites. Our favourite was **Beaupre Castle** (pronounced bewper) , an Elizabethan country house cum fortress set in peaceful countryside south east of Cowbridge. One of the charms of Beaupre is its location, a little way off the road accessible by a footpath across green fields. The walk takes (only a few minutes, and we were rewarded by having the castle all to ourselves. A particularly attractive feature worth looking out for is the beautifully carved outer porch, dated 1586. It bears the arms of the Bassetts, the family linked with Beaupre since medieval times, and their motto (in Welsh) 'Better Death than Shame'.

From Beaupre we made our way westwards through country lanes through **Llandow** and discovered just two miles west of the village, **Stembridge**, an impressive Grade II listed Tudor farmhouse, which makes an ideal touring base for the Vale of Glamorgan.

Stembridge, Nr Llandow, Cowbridge 0656 79389 Map Ref: 6F

This is the charming home of John and Valerie Lee, who provide bed and breakfast accommodation in three beautifully furnished, well-equipped guest rooms, each with en-suite or private bathroom. Alternatively, you can choose to stay in The Old Stable which stands adjacent to the farmhouse and has been completely refurbished to provide very comfortable, self-catering accommodation which has every modern facility for complete comfort. With an acre of beautiful gardens for guests use and many scenic walks on the doorstep, Stembridge is perfect for a relaxing and peaceful holiday.

Glamorgan's coast, like its countryside, is full of contrasts. **Barry Island,** for example, is a bright and breezy traditional seaside resort where children enjoy all the fun of the fair. Yet close by there are spectacular views from towering cliffs looking out across the Bristol Channel to the Devon coast. A little way inland, close to **Penmark**, we spent an enjoyable morning looking over the ruined castle of **Umfrevilles** and the superb Norman Church of St. Mary, one of the largest in the Vale of Glamorgan. How the village got its name is uncertain, but we were told a colourful story. It is suggested that Penmark is the Anglicised version of "Pen March", the horse's head. In King Arthur's time, a prince of North Wales owned a very strong and very swift horse, which was used to carry messages to the king's court in Somerset. On one occasion the horse was galloping so fast it slipped, and in falling was decapitated, at a place called **Cefn March,** "the horse's ridge", near **Gilfach Reda** in Cardiganshire. Its head, however, travelled on until it fell, and the place where it fell became known as "Pen March".

The **B4265** took us to **Llantwit Major.** We love looking around old

---

Did You Know...
There is a full
Town and Village Index
at the back of the book?

---

churches, so Llantwit Major was a special delight for us. In a sheltered hollow below the town's crooked old streets we came across a huge church of cathedral like proportions. **The Church of St Illtud** was, in fact, a religious site which in many ways had the stature of a cathedral. It was founded in around A.D. 500 by St. Illtud, an influential early Christain figure, and St. David, Wales's patron saint, is known to have studied here. In medieval times the church grew to its present dimensions we found out that it is, in reality, two churches in one, since it is a combination of an early Norman and late 13th century church. We spent a great deal of time exploring this cavernous church, and were most impressed by its fine collection of Celtic crosses and pillars inscribed with the most intricate designs.

In a tranquil location in Llantwit Major, **West House Country Hotel** lies on the edge of the Heritage Coast and is a beautifully appointed and well-run establishment where a relaxing country house atmosphere combines with the facilities one associates with a top city hotel. The 21 en-suite guest rooms have every modern amenity and like the rest of the hotel, are furnished and decorated to designer standards. The sunny conservatory provides the perfect setting for morning coffee or afternoon tea whilst the elegant Heritage Restaurant offers the discerning guest a choice of both à la carte and

Nash Point.

table d'hôte menus, each providing an extensive selection of fine cuisine at surprisingly reasonable prices, accompanied by a carefully selected wine list.

West House Country Hotel, Llantwit Major 0446 792406
(Fax: 0446 796147) Map Ref: 6F

Acorn Camping and Caravanning is a delightful hilltop campsite lying just minutes from the town centre of Llantwit Major, from where it is signposted. Three years ago, Acorn represented a dream come true for the Bradleys, who bought it having been keen caravanners themselves for over twenty years. Set in four and a half acres, this is a super touring base, within easy reach of many local attractions and surrounded by beautiful countryside, ideal for walking. Pitches are all well-spaced, some with electric hook-ups, and static caravans are also available for hire. Facilities include a toilet and shower block, site shop for those essential items and a public telephone. Children can safely play in the recreation area, whilst the games room proves popular with older children, making this a site for the whole family.

Acorn Camping and Caravanning, Llantwit Major
0446 794024 / 0703 474718 Map Ref: 6E

Nash Point, is a headland with two lighthouses and the remnants of an Iron Age fort. The cliffs along this part of the coast are made up of huge slabs of limestone which have weathered in a peculiar way to resemble giant building blocks. Nearby is **St. Donats Castle**, the home of the Atlantic College in which first Lord Mountbatten and now the Prince of Wales have taken great interest and given their support. The castle, which dates from about 1300, was owned by American newspaper magnate William Randolph Hearst who spent huge sums restoring and furnishing the historic building. His guests here included film stars and VIPs from all over the world. The castle now houses the United World College of the Atlantic, the world's first international sixth form school with students from many countries.

In nearby Marcross we found **The Horse Shoe Inn,** built over one hundred years ago but recently renovated by the present landlord, Vic Dawes. It has warm, open bars and tucked away upstairs is a pool room with a juke box, a favourite spot for youngsters. Outside you can enjoy both your drink and a bar meal in the pleasant garden which has a large lawn. Food is available at lunchtime only, but Joanne and Vic Dawes make sure you will not forget the good food they provide. Apart from main meals, there is a wide selection of snacks available all at equally reasonable prices.

Situated only a half mile from Nashpoint Lighthouse and the rocky shoreline that surrounds it; The Horseshoe Inn has two, comfortable double rooms available for those tempted to stay longer in this pleasant area.

The Horseshoe Inn, Marcross 0656 69945 Map Ref: 6E

We followed the coast road around to **Ogmore**, a pretty village on the mouth of the Ogmore River. A short distance upstream, we came to a tributary the River Ewenny which flows into the Ogmore. Guarding a ford across the Ewenny are the ruins of **Ogmore Castle**, a stronghold of the Norman de Londres family. We stayed on the

B4524 for **Ewenny,** for we had bee told in no uncertain terms that we must visit its ancient priory. We weren't disappointed, for the priory which, like Ogmore Castle, is located on the banks of the river was fascinating. It seemed, to us, to represent a strange mixture of the religious and the military. The medieval church, which appeared to be fortified, was founded by William de Londres of Ogmore Castle in the early 12th century. Its precinct walls, with their towers and gateways, give the priory its unlikely military character, though experts tell us that they were put up for reasons of prestige rather than defence. Altogether a most intriguing site!

The Haywain, at Coychurch is a stone farmhouse, approximately one hundred years old has only been a public house for the past ten years. Inside the bar is spacious and comfortable, with tapestry upholstered furnishings. It is a Courage pub, serving the brewery's best beers as well as catering for the hungry. Every day there are thirteen hot, home cooked dishes to choose from. Children are well catered for, and when fed and content, can play in the large garden where a painted wagon is waiting to be explored as well as swings and climbing frames. Part of the garden is a plum orchard with about 20 plum trees. Homemade jam is produced, which you can buy, and plum puddings are a house speciality.

The Haywain, Coychurch 0656 79568 Map Ref: 5F

From here, it was just a short journey to Bridgend, known in Welsh as ' Pen-y-Bont ar Ogwr' - the crossing of the River Ogmore. Once regarded as a vital enough route for the construction of two castles on either side of the river. The surviving remains can be found on the west side of the river in the area known as Newcastle

Two miles east of Bridgend, just off the **A473,** in **Coychurch.** Enjoying a peaceful hillside setting just outside the village, **Coed-y-Mwstwr** is a superb Victorian country house hotel, ideal for that romantic break away or a 'spoil yourself' weekend. Set within seventeen acres of well-laid out gardens and woodland, this impressive establishment combines the highest standards of service and facilities with a warm and relaxing period ambience. The twenty three en-suite guest rooms are all superbly equipped and surprisingly spacious, with attention to detail ensuring maximum comfort. Coed-y-Mwstwr has a well-deserved reputation for its excellent restaurant which is open to non-residents and has earned the coveted AA Two Rosettes award. Here you can savour a varied menu of the finest fresh local produce, imaginatively prepared and beautifully presented, accompanied by a fine selection of wines.

Coed-y-Mwstwr, Coychurch, Near Bridgend 0656 863122 Map Ref: 5F

We then rejoined the M4 motorway and drove to **Swansea**, Wales's second city. Our images of Swansea were coloured by the writings of **Dylan Thomas**, who was born and raised in the Uplands area of the city. He described Swansea an 'ugly, lovely town' more the former than the latter, we assumed, bearing in mind the poet's inclinations to paint an evocative picture of his home town. We were wrong. Swansea is an attractive city indeed, parts of it are very attractive. Much of the Swansea of Dylan Thomas's youth was destroyed by German bombs during the last war. The city centre is modern and quite pleasant, but the place that really impressed us was the **Maritime Quarter.**

Marinas and waterfront developments are all the rage in Britain nowadays. In our travels we have seen some good examples of marina development and some bad examples. Swansea's new Maritime Quarter is one of the best. The centrepiece of the development is the old dock, now transformed into a marina and surrounded by stylish waterfront buildings. When you're strolling around this area, look out for the modernistic pieces of themed sculpture on the walls and by the walkways, which contribute further to the charm of this well thought out, architecturally adventurous development.

Swansea.

A former warehouse on the waterfront has been converted into a **Maritime and Industrial Museum,** which traces the development of Swansea as a port. Upstairs, we were surprised to come across a complete woollen mill in working order which still produces traditional Welsh weaves. Swansea is an appealing blend of traditional and modern. Unlike Cardiff, you'll occasionally hear Welsh spoken as a first language in the streets. 'Old' Swansea also lives on in the city's covered market, which is probably the best fresh foods market in Wales. We couldn't resist a jar of cockles, freshly picked from the nearby Penclawdd cockle beds on the Gower Peninsula. We were, however, a little dubious about trying laverbread, that unique Welsh delicacy which looks like a most unappetising black paste. It is, we were assured, a most tasty accompaniment to bacon and eggs, though we found it difficult to forget the fact that it is made of seaweed!

Another most appealing feature of Swansea is its setting. Dylan Thomas described gazing down over the rooftops from his hillside home to a Swansea 'by the side of a long and splendidly curving shore'. We have always been fans of his writing especially the works that describe his childhood so endeavoured to find the house in which he was born. He wrote that 'you've got to be a Sherpa' to get to his home - 5 Cwmdonkin Drive. He was right, for Cwmdonkin Drive is a very steep street and his house, of course, is not far from the top! The house, an ordinary looking semi detached, is still in private ownership, though it does bear a blue plaque with the simple inscription 'Dylan Thomas, Poet, 1914 - 53. Born in this house'.

Tredilion House Hotel, Swansea 0792 470766 (Fax : 0792 456064)
Map Ref : 4C

For the discerning guest **Tredilion House Hotel** which lies just outside Swansea on the Gower road, makes a superior holiday base and carries a Three Crown Highly Commended rating. Converted from a late Victorian house, Tredilion has lost none of its original

Gower Peninsula, Worms Head.

character and the superb period furnishings and carefully co-ordinated decor enhance its natural beauty. The seven en-suite guest rooms are of a standard commensurate with a top city hotel, each providing full facilities and Dorothy Mesner is a friendly hostess whose professional expertise makes everything look easy. Dining is a treat, with a choice full or continental breakfast and a mouthwatering dinner menu which is complemented by a fine wine list.

Dylan Thomas spent enjoyable days as a young man on the nearby **Gower Peninsula** and that's where we headed for next. First, we passed through strangely named **The Mumbles**, a small sailing and watersports centre along Swansea Bay. Situated in the heart of Mumbles bay and within fifteen minutes of the Gower, **Tides Reach** is a beautiful early Victorian guest house run by charming hostess Jan Maybery. All the reception rooms are beautifully furnished with William IV and Regency furniture and the lovely high ceilings create an air of light and space. The seven guest rooms are simply delightful, three with en-suite facilities and some offering wonderful sea views. Breakfast is a treat, with a wide selection of dishes. During your stay, you would be well-advised to pay a visit to Maybery Antiques on Brandy Cove Road, Bishopston, which is Jan's own shop. She specialises in beautiful porcelain, lovely antique furniture and works by local artists.

Tides Reach Guest House, Mumbles, Swansea 0792 404877 Map Ref: 4C

Beyond The Mumbles lies the lovely Gower Peninsula, quite rightly designated as an 'Area of Outstanding Natural Beauty'. Gower's southern coast is made up of a succession of sandy, sheltered bays. The first of these, **Langland Bay**, is just around the headland from The Mumbles, a short distance from Newton. Further along you'll come to **Nicholaston**, where situated on the south slopes of **Cefn Bryn** and overlooking Oxwich Bay, the **Nicholaston House Hotel** is an impressive castellated mansion dating back to 1887. This is a tranquil haven, set within beautiful gardens and offering a wealth

84

of wildlife and lovely country walks close by. The twelve en-suite guest rooms are very tastefully furnished and boast wonderful countryside and sea views. Downstairs you can enjoy a refreshing drink in the convivial atmosphere of the bar lounge, practice some shots in the snooker room, or simply relax and admire the views from the lawned terrace. In the newly refurbished restaurant, dining is a real treat, with each tempting dish qualifying as a 'Taste of Wales', which means it has been freshly prepared from the finest local produce.

Nicholaston House Hotel, Nicholaston, Gower 0792 371317 Map Ref: 4B

One of the prettiest Gower villages is **Oxwich,** which is huddled along one lane at the west end of a superb three miles of sand. It was once a small port exporting limestone and a haven for smugglers. Today is it a wonderful holiday area with safe bathing from a clean beach, wind surfing and water skiing. Just back from the beach is part of the Oxwich National Nature Reserve, home of many rare species of orchid as well as other plant life. There are many species of birds too which delight ornithologists. In the village are some picturesque cottages in traditional Gower style including John Wesley's cottage.

Oxwich Bay Hotel, Oxwich, Gower 0792 390329 Map Ref: 4A

Oxwich Bay Hotel enjoys an enviable location, set within eight acres of grounds on the shores of Oxwich Bay itself. This is the perfect setting for a peaceful holiday in beautiful surroundings, with lovely gardens set against a backdrop of wooded cliffs and overlooking a golden sandy beach. There is a happy family atmosphere here and the high standards of professionalism make everything seem easy. The thirteen guest rooms are all en-suite and provide every modern facility for maximum comfort, whilst downstairs the attractive restaurant boasts windows on all sides and provides a lovely setting in which to savour the excellent menu and wine list. With a variety of watersports and other activities readily available, Oxwich Bay Hotel is the ideal holiday base.

Oxwich also contains a lovely church, **St Illtyd's,** which lies half hidden by trees but go and seek it out. It is though that its ancient font was bought to the church by St Illtyd. For walkers there are plenty of footpaths to explore. The walk to Oxwich Point provides some magnificent views of Gower .

Close by and down a steep hill lies **Port Eynon**, now regarded as something of a surfing centre. This attractive hamlet lies close to some rather spectacular coastline from where you can see the coasts of Somerset and Devon. Set in the heart of the ancient village of Port Eynon, **Borva Cottage** is a secluded haven, home of Wenda and John Hancock who invite you to relax in the peaceful surrounds of their patio courtyard and Victorian garden. This is a very special place where guests are encouraged to take life easy and soak up the lovely country cottage atmosphere. There are three well equipped character bedrooms, beautifully decorated with sloping ceilings and varying window levels adding to their appeal. After a refreshing night's sleep you can savour a wholesome breakfast to a backdrop of birdsong and views over the lovely garden. With a golden beach just two minutes walk away, it seems your quiet break away is complete.

Borva Cottage, Port Eynon 0792 390498 Map Ref: 5A

Our penultimate stop in this delightful area was made in **Llangennith.** Here you'll find the largest church on the peninsula, dating from the 12th century. It is on the site of a 6th century priory founded by St Cenydd but sacked by Viking raiders in AD 986. The grave inside is thought to be St Cenydds. The church tower has a saddle back roof, an excellent example of fortified architecture that was once typical in the area. The nearby **Llanmadoc Hill** is worth the effort for the views it affords and on its lower slopes the **Bulwark** is an Iron Age hillfort.

The hub of the pretty coastal village of Llangennith is without doubt the **Kings Head** pub, a very old country inn standing opposite the ancient Norman church. Ownership of this lovely inn can be traced back to 1790 and long before that, it was a farm and brewery dating back to the settlement of St. Cennyd, a Cornish Saint of the 7th century. Today, Anna and Paul Stevens serve the finest Real Ale and superb food, with delicious pizzas made to order and a wide selection of local seafood as well as traditional desserts such as Spotted Dick. The beach below the village is three miles of the finest sand with Rhossili Downs rolling away to the east making this a delightful place to while away an afternoon.

Kings Head, Llangennith, Gower 0792 386212 Map Ref: 4A

As a fitting climax to our visit to this part of Wales, we went to the westernmost tip of both the Gower Peninsula and West Glamorgan. Gower ends at **Worms Head,** a spectacular spindly island connected to the mainland by a low tide causeway - make sure to check the times of the tides before setting out on the walk to Worms Head if you want to avoid being stranded! Windy Worms Head is reached from the clifftop village of **Rhossili,** which looks out over a huge, sandy, west facing beach popular with surfers Dylan Thomas described it as 'miles of yellow coldness going away into the distance of the sea'.

Rhossili Farmhouse is possibly the oldest house in Rhossili and lies opposite the church just a minute from the car park. It is here that two ex-teachers, Gary Ley and Helen Sinclair have established Sculpture Culture, a unique sculpture studio. Helen trained in sculpture at Wimbledon School of Art and is gaining an international reputation for her superb work. Until five years ago, when they set up the studio, Gary was a complete newcomer to sculpture, but through the excellent tuition of both Helen and renowned professional sculptor, John Oakman, he now works alongside Helen. They make a good team, with Helen sculpting, Gary casting and both sharing the task of mould-making. For handcrafted, individually designed garden and house sculptures, this is definitely the place to look.

Sculpture Culture, Rhossili Farmhouse, Rhossili 0792 390798
Map Ref: 4A

We are always attracted to churches, so spent some time wandering around the sturdy little church here. We said at the start of this chapter that this part of South Wales was full of surprises - well, we found another one at Rhosili when we discovered a memorial plaque in the church to a Gower man, Edgar Evans, better known perhaps as Petty Officer Evans who died in the tragic expedition to the Antarctic led by Captain Scott in 1912.

CHAPTER THREE

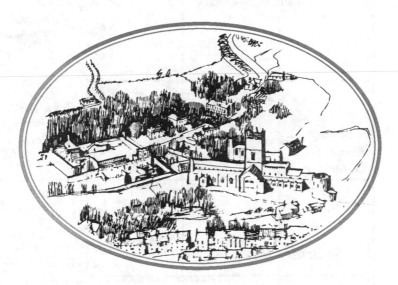

South West Wales.

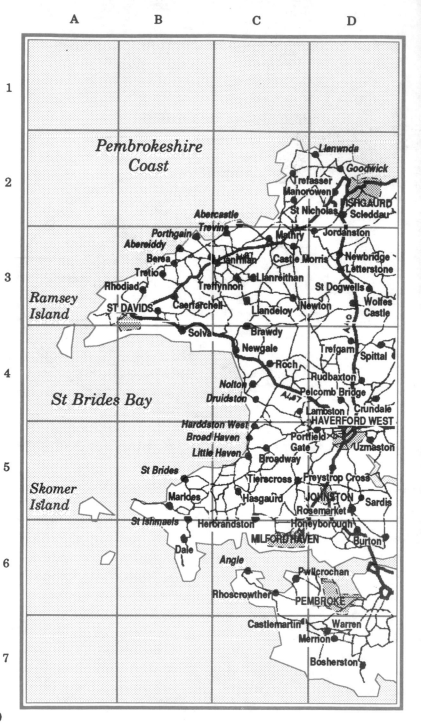

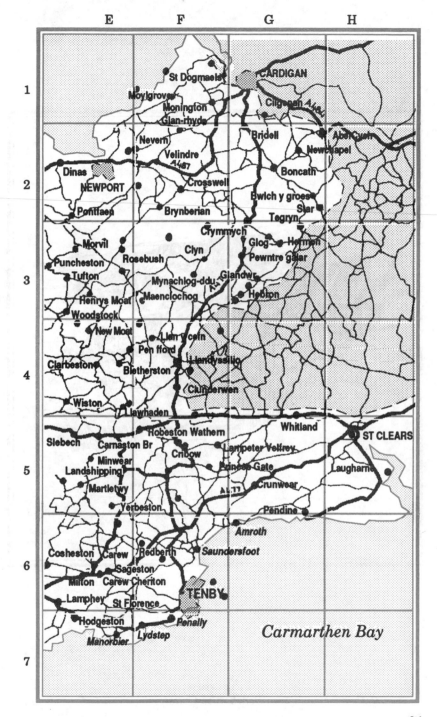

Carmarthen Bay

Pembroke Coast.

CHAPTER THREE

South West Wales.

One feature, above all else, dominates this part of Wales. It is the magnificent Pembrokeshire Coast National Park, Britain's only coastal based National Park and one of the most spectacular stretches of coastal natural beauty in Europe. We had spent holidays here in the past, so were looking forward to renewing our acquaintance with this lovely part of Wales and exploring it thoroughly for the first time. We weren't disappointed by what we found. In the time we spent in Wales's southwest we discovered huge beaches and tiny, secluded coves, cliffs and headlands ablaze with wild flowers and were even lucky enough to spot seals basking on the rocks. The Pembrokeshire Coast National Park is 180 miles long. Its starting point on the southfacing shoreline is Amroth, near Tenby. The park then runs right the way around the ruggedly beautiful southwestern tip of Wales and up along the northfacing coast almost to Cardigan. Walking enthusiasts sing the praises of Pembrokeshire, for there's a long distance footpath which travels almost the entire length of the National Park. You don't have to be a member of the superfit stoutbooted brigade to enjoy this path. Most visitors, as we soon discovered, are content to walk short stretches of it that's what we did, and on our way spotted a greater variety of seabird than we'd ever seen before (in the skies around the cliffs west of Tenby, for example, we saw guillemots, cormorants and oystercatchers). Pembrokeshire really is a birdwatcher's paradise it's little wonder that the National Park has adopted the razorbill as its official symbol.

We need to explain a few things about Pembrokeshire at the start of this chapter. The name Pembrokeshire has taken a bit of a battering in the hands of government reorganisers in the last 15 years or so. The old county of Pembrokeshire was swallowed up when the huge new supercounty of Dyfed was created in 1974. Many of the locals were none too happy about that, and helped perpetuate the name by using it within the newly created Preseli Pembrokeshire District Council in the north and its neighbour, the South Pembrokeshire District Council. The name also survives because of its associations with the National Park. So Pembrokeshire thankfully lives on. People still talk of going to Pembrokeshire or of coming from Pembrokeshire, and always use it when addressing letters. Its identity as a county may have ceased to exist officially it's just that no one has taken any notice of the civil servants! As we write moves are being made to revert back to Pembrokeshire. Local traditions are important in this corner of Wales. South Pembrokeshire, for example, still has a reputation of being the little England beyond Wales because of its English speaking population and Anglicised placenames, while north Pembrokeshire clings to its Welsh language and different customs.

We don't want to give the impression that this chapter is dedicated entirely to Pembrokeshire. Before reaching the National Park, we travelled through pastoral green countryside south of **Carmarthen**, and spent some time on the sweeping, sandy shores of Carmarthen Bay. Our first stop was the **Pembrey Country Park**. This is a most unusual place mixture of pine forest, sand dune and huge beach. The beach, no less than seven miles long, is known as Cefn Sidan. When we were there, we were fortunate enough to be able to watch sand yachts racing up and down this seemingly endless stretch of beach. Pembrey's strange forest beside the sea, which was planted to help stabilise the dunes, can be explored by following waymarked footpaths or from the saddle of a pony. The park also has a narrowgauge railway, dry skislope, children's play areas and picnic sites.

Before leaving the area, we drove the few miles to **Kidwelly**, where we visited well preserved **Kidwelly Castle**. Another of those little known Welsh fortresses that merit much greater public acclaim has a formidable, twin towered gatehouse that still sends shivers down the spine. We were also directed to the outskirts of the town where the **Kidwelly Industrial Museum** is located. Kidwelly was once an important tinplate manufacturer and has preserved the old works as a museum where you can see furnaces, steam engines and metal cutters that resemble giant tin openers.

We drove up beside the Towy Estuary to **Carmarthen**, now the main administrative centre for the new supercounty of Dyfed that we mentioned earlier. But that doesn't mean that it's a place of anonymous modern office blocks. Far from it. Carmarthen is as Welsh as they come, especially on a Wednesday when its huge livestock market is in full swing. The green hills and vales around Carmarthen are classic Welsh farming country. On Wednesdays, it seems as if every truck, jeep and Land Rover in West Wales has made a beeline for Carmarthen's auction yards. If you've never witnessed a hectic livestock auction, you'll be taken aback. We could hardly keep up with the rapidfire speech of the auctioneer, nor could we identify who was actually making the bidding, which seemed to be based on a canny nod or a wink from members of the packed crowd to the auctioneer's rostrum or even a scratch on the nose, as far as we could tell! Everyone seemed to know what was going on except ourselves, but it was still a most entertaining experience. We also spent time exploring the historic old town, which grew up around a medieval castle overlooking the Towy.

Carmarthen, Kidwelly Castle.

Unfortunately, there's not much left of the castle today, though you can still walk through its gatehouse which looks a little lost standing as it does close to the shops and busy streets.

Tucked down a narrow alleyway called Jacksons Lane, off King Street in Carmarthen, you will discover **Y Gegin**, a delightful licensed restaurant run by welcoming hostess Brenda Richards. Dating back some 200 years, Y Gegin is a warm and inviting establishment the result of the successful conversion of three former shops. Here in immaculate surroundings, you can choose from an extensive menu which caters for everything from breakfasts and morning coffees to full lunches and tempting cream teas. For those in a hurry, there is also a take-away service available. Open Monday to Saturday from 8.00am - 6.00pm, Y Gegin is a 'hidden place' well worth seeking out, where welcome refreshment is provided throughout the day.

Y Gegin, Carmarthen 0267 231003

If legend is to be believed, Carmarthen was Merlin's City. One legend associated with the town has thankfully turned out to be untrue. Carmarthen's inhabitants are eternally grateful that the prophesy concerning Merlin's Oak proved to be incorrect. The wizened old tree stump was removed during a roadwidening scheme, despite the threat: When Merlin's Oak shall tumble down, then shall fall Carmarthen town. We are always looking, in our travels, for the unusual, the unknown and the hidden. On the eastern outskirts of Carmarthen we certainly found something that fits those descriptions. In a grassy knoll below a row of houses we discovered a Roman amphitheatre, one of only seven known in Britain. The Romans pushed no further west than Carmarthen, establishing an important base here, most of which lies buried beneath the modern town. A little further out of town, on the A40 eastwards, is the **Carmarthen Museum**. Based at a lovely old house which was previously a **Palace of the Bishop of St David's**, the museum has a wide range of exhibits. We could have spent many hours browsing around the rooms, which were full of fascinating exhibits Roman finds, items

96

from ancient Egypt, domestic exhibits from rural Wales, costumes, and even a pennyfarthing, to name but a few.

There is a multitude of choice when trying to decide where to stay in the area. To ease that choice we reccomend the following. **Glog Farm**, just ten minutes from the town and also near to the quiet sandy beach and castle at Llanstephan, is a small forty acre farm with very comfortable accommodation with a Welsh Tourist Board award. The farm has two family rooms, one ensuite, and three smaller bedrooms, all have hand wash basins, soap and towels. In addition there are two shower and toilet rooms. Early morning tea is brought to your room three quarters of an hour before breakfast of your choice is served. In the evening you can enjoy a four course dinner from a choice of menu. If you solitude, there are two lounges where you can read or watch TV. Maureen Gribble works hard to make sure that all her guests are well cared for and she will willingly fill flasks for you to take out or provide you with a packed lunch on request. To get to Glog leave Carmarthen on the A40, westbound. In a quarter of a mile turn left on to the **B4312** which is signposted Llansteffan. Follow this road for about four miles, turn right to Llangynog - Glog is now signposted and turn right into the farm drive after about half a mile.

Glog Farm, Llansteffan 026783 271

Self-catering enthusiasts will discover a real haven at **Pontgarreg Farm**, a 'hidden' place tucked away in the tranquil village of **Johnstown**. From Carmarthen, take the road to Johnstown and in the village turn down the road which says 'Dead End' - the farm lies about half a mile up on the right. The charming home of Monica and John Davies, Pontgarreg itself is over 400 years old and was once owned by local hero General Nott, a big statue of whom still stands in the centre of Carmarthen. There are five fully equipped and beautifully furnished self-contained units, three in the Grade II listed barn conversion and two in separate bungalows. Surrounded by 65 acres, peace and tranquility are assured, yet Carmarthen is only a short drive away.

Pontgarreg Farm, Johnstown, Carmarthen 0267 237751

Travelling on the westbound carriageway from Carmarthen towards **St. Clears** turning you will discover a simply delightful place to stay. **Montclare,** the charming home of Mrs Pat Jones sits directly alongside the **A40.** Set within large, well stocked gardens this attractive 1930's house provides a relaxing and peaceful holiday base.

Montclare, St. Clears, Carmarthen 0994 230236

Within the house every room is a picture, with oak supplied from two ships, the S.S. Montrose and the S.S. Montclare, a major feature throughout. The dining room boasts the original walls from the cabin on the S.S. Montrose, where Dr. Crippen was actually arrested! With two beautifully furnished guest rooms, one en-suite, it comes as no surprise to learn that Montclare carries the high accolade of the Wales Tourist Board's Two-crown De Luxe award.

On the same road we discovered that guests at **Trebersed Farmhouse** will find a warm welcome awaits them from friendly hosts Rosemary and David Jones. When taking the A40 out of Carmarthen towards St. Clears, after about 1 mile, turn right and following this road up the hill, the entrance to Trebersed can be found on the right. Part of a 170 acre working dairy farm this charming 17th century house once came within the Manor of Thriskberkett and although it has been extended and modernised, still retains all its original character. Exposed brick walls and beamed ceilings add to its charm and accommodation for non-smokers is provided in two attractive, well-equipped en-suite guest rooms. However, arguably the best feature of this lovely place is its peaceful countryside location, high above Carmarthen offering beautiful views all around.

Trebersed Travellers Rest, Carmarthen 0267 238182

St.Clears has some claims to fame in Owain Glyndwr who suffered defeat here in 1406 at the hands of the Pembrokeshires army. The village also featured in the Rebbecca Riots during the 1840's,where rioters with greivances similiar to those of the Chartists,destroyed tollgates.Reform was eventually introduced in 1884 and no tollgates were left in South Wales.

Travelling through St. Clears on the old A40 road from Carmarthen, if you turn right at the traffic lights at the end of the town, signposted Pwll-Trap, a mile further on you will come to **The White Lion Inn** on your left. This attractive 18th century freehouse welcomes families and makes an ideal stopping-off point in any journey. Keith and Ann Major are friendly hosts who have created a special place where you can enjoy fine ale, first class food and comfortable accommodation. The extensive blackboard menu offers a range of hot and cold meals, including homemade pies and for guests wishing to stay, accommodation is provided in four very comfortable bedrooms, one with en-suite bathroom.

The White Lion Inn, Pwll-Trap, St. Clears 0994 230370 Map Ref: 5H

One place well worth calling in at is **The Butchers Arms** on the road to **Laugharne** from St. Clears. It can be reached by turning left at the traffic lights in St. Clears onto the **A4066**. It is on the left a short distance after the flyover. Recently taken over by Lesley Dempsey and her son Andrew, this lovely 18th century pub is full of atmosphere. You can relax whilst savouring fine cask ale and a tasty bar snack, but the highlight of a visit here is the superb restaurant where exposed stone walls, and oak beams go hand in hand with cosy candlelit tables to provide the perfect setting in which to savour a mouthwatering menu freshly prepared by Andrew who is an experienced chef.

The Butchers Arms, St. Clears 0994 231069 Map Ref: 5H

The rich farmlands in these parts inspired some of Dylan Thomas's most evocative writing. We had already made our pilgrimage to Dylan's birthplace in Swansea (see Chapter Two), and wanted to complete the picture of the poet's life by visiting sleepy Laugharne. It was here, in The Boathouse, that Dylan wrote some of his greatest works. He discovered the obscure little seatown in the 1940s, spending one of the happiest periods of his life here beside its heronpriested shore. This timeless, mild, beguiling island of a town provided much of the inspiration for his best known work, 'Under Milk Wood', a day in the life of his imaginary village of Llareggub (spell it backwards!). Dylan Thomas, no stranger to destructive drinking sprees, died aged only thirty nine in New York in 1953. A plain white cross in Laugharne's churchyard marks his final resting place, and **The Boathouse** is now a museum dedicated to his life and work.

Lovers of Dylan Thomas country will find a simply lovely place to stay at **Halldown**, the charming home of Thomas and Helen Best. Situated close to the small village of Laugharne this lovely farmhouse is over 200 years old and is set in one and a half acres of land, a safe haven for children to play in. Inside, the house is full of character, a particular feature being the exposed stone wall in the lounge housing a large fireplace which offers welcome warmth during the winter months. The five guest rooms are very comfortable, with attractively co-ordinated furnishings and each is named after a local river. Helen, an auxiliary nurse for many years, is a warm, welcoming hostess and whilst here you may discover her unusual hobby - collecting stones!

Halldown, Cross Inn, Near Laugharne, Dyfed 0994 21452   Map Ref: 5H

We had become completely seduced by Laugharne's soothing, unhurried atmosphere. We enjoyed the simple pleasures of wandering past its seafront castle and through its reassuringly oldfashioned streets, and in our exploration came across **Laugharne Park**, one of the most beautiful places we have ever seen. We found more endless stretches of sand at nearby **Pendine**, which was used for landspeed records in the 1920s by Sir Malcolm Campbell and others. In 1924, Sir Malcolm broke the World Motor Flying Kilometre Record by averaging 146 mph at Pendine. But soon afterwards tragedy struck. While attempting to beat Sir Malcolm, Welshman J.G. Parry Thomas was killed in an accident on the beach. His car, Babs was buried in the sands for forty two years before being dug up for restoration in 1969.

Hazell Well Farm, called **Ffynnoncyll** in Welsh, is a comfortable old stone farmhouse sitting on the side of a hill. The house is reached by a mile long farm track from the road and is surrounded by its own land which includes mature woodlands. The woods on steep slopes, are a wonderful place for children and adults to explore. There are two comfortable guest rooms which offer you the chance of staying in this idyllic setting and if you are disabled, you will find that everything possible has been done to make you welcome. One of the owners is

Laugharne.

wheelchair bound and understanding the issues of access has had installed a Stannah stair lift, a ramped entrance and every door wheelchair width. Breakfast and evening meals are available which you enjoy from the dining room which has marvellous views across the valley. Hazell Well is a family run farm with horses and ponies. Anne and Mervyn Dunham are people who give their guests the freedom of the land, providing they are sensible and follow the country code. Guests are always welcome to watch or help with the daily farming round. The Dunhams offer riding holidays as well, which are tailored to each guest's need. The farmhouse also has an annexe where you can enjoy a self catering holiday. To find Hazell Well Farm, enter Whitland on the A40. Turn onto the **B4328** to **Tavernspite**. Follow this road for approximately two miles to a junction, signposted to Ciffig Church. Take the left fork and follow it round to the church on the right. Past the church a few hundred yards on the left, you will see a white farm. Just in front of the farm there is a farm track which is hard to see. Take this and follow it down for a mile approximately and the Hazellwell is in front of you.

Hazell Well Farm, Whitland Map Ref: 4G

We found that there are lots of other attractive places to stay in this area. From Pendine we followed the **B4314,** then the **B4328** to **Whitland** where we found set in over one hundred acres of truly outstanding countryside the **Preseli Country House Hotel.** By the **A478** Cardigan to Tenby road the hotel offers that special something that money just cannot buy.

Preseli Country House Hotel, Whitland 09947 425 Map Ref: 4G

Home of no less than three Grand National winners, this outstanding establishment now belongs to friendly hostess Noreen Vaughan who regularly welcomes major pop music bands into her superb recording studios. But don't be put off, this is most definitely not a noisy place to stay, as the tranquil surroundings will prove. The six guest rooms are all en-suite with beautiful period and antique furnishings enhancing their character and charm. Noreen immediately makes you feel as though you are staying at a friend's house and her excellent cooking caters for both simple and Cordon Bleu tastes, all of which ensures a memorable stay for her many guests.

Returning to the coast, we drove though **Amroth** - which marks the start of the **Pembrokeshire Coast National Park** - to **Saundersfoot**. Everything in Saundersfoot revolves around its harbour, which is packed with colourful sailing craft in summer. The resort, which has an attractive sandy beach, is probably the busiest watersports centre in South Wales. **Edgecombe Guest House,** is a family guest house run by Lilian Lang and her husband, has ten guest rooms, four of which are ensuite, and all have central heating, hand basins with hot and cold water, and shaving points. Children are welcome and there are several family rooms, most of which have wonderful panoramic views of the beach and the harbour. A ground floor ensuite bedroom is ideal for disabled people who are welcome at Edgecombe. Baby sitting can be arranged, and cots and high chairs are available.

There is a heated swimming pool surrounded by a patio with flower borders and established trees. Lilian's husband is a qualified A.S.A. swimming instructor who runs special learning to swim and stroke improvement classs every week, for either children or adults. Drinks and bar snacks are available during the day either on the patio, by the swimming pool or in the bar. Evening meals are available from a set menu of homecooked meals all served with fresh vegetables. From Saundersfoot village fields and woodlands stretch right down to the beach and the Pembrokeshire coastal path starts and ends here.

Edgecombe Guest House, Saundersfoot 0834 812810 Map Ref: 6F

Lying just three miles outside **Tenby,** in this picturesque village and enjoying a superb location overlooking the sea, you will find a lovely place to stay at the **Merlewood Hotel** on St. Brides Hill, which carries a Wales Tourist Board 3-Crown Commended rating.

Merlewood Hotel, St. Brides Hill, Saundersfoot 0834 812421 Map Ref: 6F

This is a perfect example of a holidaymaker's haven, with excellent facilities including a heated outdoor swimming pool, childrens' play area, pool table, nine-hole putting green and, for your convenience, a small launderette. The hotel bedrooms provide every modern facility, including en-suite bath or shower, whilst the dining room offers an extensive menu both at breakfast and dinner. All this plus the beach only minutes away, make this a lovely place to stay.

Before leaving the area, we took a short drive to **Wiseman's Bridge** which has a pretty beach used for a rehearsal of the D - Day landings watched over by Winston Churchill. Then it was on to Saundersfoot's next door neighbour **Tenby,** the most popular resort in Pembrokeshire. We soon fell under Tenby's spell, despite the narrow medieval streets which aren't really meant for the motor car.

Situated in a quiet 'floral' street in the heart of historic Tenby, just yards from the town's beautiful golden sands, **Ripley St. Marys Hotel** makes an ideal holiday base. Friendly hosts Alan and Kath Mace have been the proud owners of this welcoming establishment for over 20 years and offer first class hospitality and excellent homecooked food. Alan is a former Mayor of Tenby, the direct line of which goes back to 1402 by Royal Charter! Within the hotel there are fourteen comfortable and well-equipped guest rooms, eight with en-suite bathroom. You can relax with a drink in the Residents' Bar Lounge before making your way to the attractive dining room, and to end the day, what could be nicer than a stroll along the beach?

Ripley St. Marys Hotel, Tenby 0834 842837 Map Ref: 6F

Tenby's charming medieval character together with its crooked lanes leading down to a picturesque harbour were the things that really impressed us about this resort. It's a popular place in its own right, without having to rely on candy floss and funfairs to attract its visitors.However we would recommend an interesting visit whilst here.

Silent World Aquarium and Wildlife Art Gallery, Tenby
0834 844498 Map Ref: 6F

An old chapel may seem an odd setting for an aquarium, but that is what you will find when you visit **Silent World Aquarium** in Tenby. Situated on the Narberth road close to North Beach car park, where visitors can park, brown signs lead you to the 19th century chapel, which houses this amazing collection of marine and aquatic life, amphibians and reptiles. Look out for the touch tank, where you will meet the likes of Belinda the Blenny, and as you gaze at the other

Tenby.

tanks, don't be fooled - there are many creatures lurking within, so take your time to see how many you can spot. Afterwards, you can relax with a cup of coffee and browse in the art gallery and gift shop which offer a wealth of wildlife paintings, books and crafts as mementos of your visit.

There's so much antiquity in Tenby. Don't miss the **Five Arches,** a fortified gate which is part of the medieval wall enclosing the old town. On the way down to the quay we came across the **Tudor Merchant's House,** a relic of Tenby's prosperous seafaring days and a fine example of a comfortable town house of about 500 years ago. We also took the short boat trip of two miles across to **Caldey Island** to visit the monastery which produces a famous range of perfumes made from the island's flower petals.

The cliffs, beaches and bays of the south Pembrokeshire coast are magnificent. We were, of course, by no means the first people to think so or to praise them on the written page. As early as the 12th century **Manorbier,** just around the headland from Tenby, was being described as the pleasantest spot in Wales. The castle here belonged Giraldus Cambrensis, Gerald of Wales, the person responsible for that flattering description. Giraldus, a monk and chronicler, wrote the first account of life in medieval Wales, in which he proved to be a keen and accurate observer of the Welsh character. The cliff scenery was at its most spectacular around **Stack Rocks** and **St Govan's Head**, where we stumbled across the tiny religious site of **St Govan's Chapel** huddling amongst the rocks almost at sea level. This minute chapel, accessible by fifty two stone steps, was built on the site of a holy well (which reputedly had miraculous healing powers) that once attracted pilgrims from far and wide.

We left the sea and seabirds and headed inland for the historic town of **Pembroke.** Like Tenby, Pembroke has well preserved medieval town walls; but the structure that dominates everything else here is the mighty castle, a truly monumental piece of military architecture which stands on a rocky crag above the river. Its Great Keep, a towering building nearly 80ft high with walls 19ft thick, is one of the most impressive of its kind in Europe. When wandering around this wonderful castle we discovered a piece of history that really surprised us: the castle was the birthplace of Harri Tudur, better known perhaps as Henry Tudor, a Welshman who defeated Richard III at the Battle of Bosworth to become Henry VII, founder of the Tudor dynasty of monarchs.

Set in four acres of woodland and lawn, off the Hollyland Road, where you can stay in comfort enjoying everything that this lovely area has to offer is **The Hollyland Hotel**. There are twelve bedrooms, all ensuite, and furnished in keeping with a house built in the late 1700's from the stone of an old church. Every room has tea/coffee making facilities, colour TV and telephone. The dining room is open to non residents, its old world atmosphere with a beamed ceiling and log fire well known and respected locally for the high standard of the cuisine. The restaurant is open until 10pm and the hotel has two bars where you can drink before you dine or enjoy coffee and liqueurs afterwards if you wish. The patio where you can sit and have morning coffee or afternoon tea would be ideal for taking photographs. The Hollyland is only a few minutes drive to some of Wale's finest beaches and for those of you who are energetic there are good golf courses, sailing and riding in the vicinity. The hotel is also just out of the town, conveniently placed for all the local attractions.

Hollyland Hotel, Pembroke 0646 681444 Map Ref: 6D

Admiral Lord Nelson regarded the **Milford Haven** waterway as one of the world's best safe and sheltered anchorages. **Pembroke Dock** was an important naval dockyard, and many fine ships were built here. Whilst here we found **The Welshmans Arms** a fully licensed free house with accommodation available in the eight rooms, four of which are ensuite. Serving real ales or wines which you can enjoy along with the variety of meals they have on offer. The 11 am to 11 pm opening hours means that you can order a meal whenever you wish during that time. With room for thirty in the restaurant you can enjoy this pub that has live music most weekends and is the meeting place of the local choir during the week. During the summer the proprietors Gerry and Jutta Aylward hold Bar -B - Q's in the beer garden for their guests.

Pembroke Castle.

The Welshmans Arm, Pembroke Dock 0646 685643 Map Ref: 6D

Pembroke Dock stands on the dividing line between the developed and undeveloped shores of the Milford Haven. Downstream there are large petrochemical plants and oil terminals, built to take advantage of the Haven's deepwater channels that can accommodate today's giant supertankers. Upstream are the tranquil, untouched creeks of the **Daugleddau**, a wooded backwater popular with bird watchers and holiday sailors.

While exploring the back lanes and eastern shores of this peaceful area, we came across the **Stanley Arms** at **Landshipping**. A pub that can be approached either by road or water has something special about it and this is what The Stanley Arms has, and more. It is an attractive building some two hundred years old, the pub was once a farmhouse and the outbuildings are still there. It was owned by a 'canny' farmer who not only ran his farm, but provided drinks in a public bar at the same time. The farm has long gone, but the drinks are still being served by a 'friendly couple', Robert and Patricia Fursse. They keep a very good house and ale to go with it. As you walk into the public bar you will see a fine natural fireplace which in winter is aglow with logs. Just off the bar is a pool room much used by the locals who regard The Stanley as a second home.

The comfortably furnished lounge bar leads you into another lounge which also has a dance floor and a small stage which is used for live music every week.We had a very pleasant lunch in the small dining area which has covers for twenty people and serves good homemade fare from a varied menu. Children are welcome to come into the pub for meals and 'special small portions' are available for them. In the public bar, which still has the original flagstone floor, you can get all manner of bar snacks from fresh rolls to 'daily specials'. The prices are very reasonable and you certainly will not leave the table hungry.

Situated in such a lovely spot, just 200 yards from the Cleddau Estuary, where there is a mooring for customer use, the local Tourism Association has appointed the pub as an information point where you can glean information from walks to birdwatching. We left The Stanley Arms feeling we had made friends and would be welcomed back next time we were there.

The Stanley Arms, Landshipping, Narberth 0834 891227 Map Ref: 5E

A couple of miles up on and situated on the main road at **Robeston Wathen**, near **Narberth, The Bush Inn** is run by a friendly couple, Eddie and Sandy Mutch who offer welcome refreshment in the form of fine ale and excellent homecooked food.

The Bush Inn, Narberth 0834 860778 Map Ref: 5E

Dating back some 100 years, this is a traditional inn, with lovely country style furnishings and oak beams enhancing the warm, friendly ambience. The pleasant lounge bar provides a relaxing setting for a quiet drink, whilst those seeking more excitement can make their way to the games room. The highlight of a visit here, however, is the extensive selection of first class food which is offered in two different menus and a variety of daily changing blackboard specials. For those warm sunny days, the beer garden to the rear, complete with play area provides an ideal lunchtime setting.

The peace and quiet of the Daugleddau could hardly have been any different to the place we visited next, even though it was only a few miles east of sleepy Landshipping. Wherever we travelled in Pembrokeshire, people had told us about **Oakwood Park**. It's an awardwinning attraction with all kinds of amusements and rides which is very professionally run, almost on the American theme park lines for example, you pay just one, all inclusive admission price which covers all the entertainment.

There's so much to see in Pembrokeshire that visitors often find it difficult to decide where to stay. One of the best compromises is an inland location close to the southern, western and northern coasts. The old county town of Haverfordwest and its pleasant rural surroundings fit the bill perfectly in this respect, for it is located more or less in the centre of Pembrokeshire.

Close by a strange, ghostly border exists which we couldn't find on any map. Known locally as the **Landsker** (or landscar), it divides the English speaking little England beyond Wales of south Pembrokeshire from the Welsh speaking north. This abrupt division of Pembrokeshire into two can be traced to early medieval times, when Norman invaders into these parts paved the way for AngloSaxon and Flemish immigrants. A line of castles was built from **Amroth** right across country to **Roch** in the far west, separating the south from the Welshry in the north. Although the Landsker is an invisible border, its significance has been profound for much of the past, it was unthinkable that marriage should take place between a man and woman from different sides of the line, even though they may have lived within a short distance of each other. We had been enchanted by the restful quality of the Daugleddau area, so decided to have a second look at it this time from its western shores. Heading along minor roads south of Haverfordwest, we first came to **Freystop.**

If first class food is what you are looking for, take a ride up Puddle Duck Hill in Freystrop village to the aptly named **Jemima's Restaurant.** Here you will find the finest local organic produce freshly prepared and beautifully presented by friendly proprietor Ann Owston. The menu is both mouthwatering and extensive with a variety to tempt the most discerning palate. Changing daily, this could easily become a regular haunt and you need never try the same thing twice. Ann grows her own herbs and soft fruits and the dessert menu often includes temptations such as Homemade Ice Cream and Primrose Pavlova. With an excellent accompanying wine list which changes quarterly, Jemima's is certainly a place not to be missed.

Jemima's Restaurant, Freystrop, Haverfordwest 0437 891109 Map Ref: 5D

After our taste of tranquillity along the Daugleddau, we had the urge really to get away from it all, so took some good advice and drove crosscountry, picking up the **B4327** towards **Dale**. Farflung Dale, in the southwestern corner of Pembrokeshire, is delightful. The little sailing and watersports centre stands at the approach to the Dale Peninsula on the mouth of the Milford Haven. We followed the road as far as we could and came to **St Ann's Head**, where a coastguard and lighthouse station keeps a close watch over dangerous, rocky shores at the entrance to the Haven. We were told to hang on to our hats, for the Dale Peninsula is one of the windiest places in Britain where gusts have been known to exceed 100 mph. But the other side of the climatic coin is Dale's sunshine record, for it is also one of the sunniest places in the country with an annual average of 1800 hours. We were lucky, for the sun was out for the entire length of our visit.

This part of Pembrokeshire is dotted with idyllic little coastal centres - they are too small to be called resorts in the usual sense of the word - which are perfect for lovers of the quieter style of seaside holidays. **Broad Haven** is another enchanting little place to stay, a popular holiday resort with a soft sandy beach which is very safe and ideal for families with small children.

Enjoying an enviable sea front location in this delightful coastal town, the **Broad Haven Hotel** is an impressive establishment, which although it can cater for over 100 guests, is still very much a family hotel, where a friendly, informal atmosphere encourages guests to mingle and make new friends. Here you will find first class accommodation with thirty six en-suite rooms each with tea and coffee

114

making facilities, colour TV (with Sky and video channel), radio and direct dial telephone. Mothers of young children are well catered for with a special room for their use, containing spin drier, tumble drier and ironing facilities. The restaurant is open to non-residents and provides an extensive and varied menu, with a choice of either the Set Menu of the day or À La Carte. There is also a late night Bistro Bar which specialises in Steak and Seafood and offers three special Theme Nights, which are Buffet, B.B.Q. and Carvery nights. Bar snacks are also available all day. The large outdoor heated swimming pool is another major attraction and has spacious sunbathing terraces, but should the sun be reluctant to shine, the hotel solarium is ideal for topping up your tan. The new addition of the soundproofed nightclub 'Scandals' is a popular evening venue with locals and visitors alike, with regular weekend entertainment including live bands, this nightclub has become the most popular place to be. The hotel also offers another bar for that peaceful quiet drink where your children are quite welcome. With three and four day breaks available as well as special weekly rates, and with the beach right over the road, it seems Broad Haven Hotel is a haven indeed!

Broad Haven Hotel, Broadhaven, Haverfordwest 0437 781366
(Fax: 0437 78107) Map Ref: 5D

Not far from Wolf's Castle on the main A40 Haverford West to Fishguard road we found **The Harp Inn** lying between the beautiful Pembrokeshire National Park and breathtaking Presceli Mountains. The proprietors Jack and Pam Sandall and their family took over the pub five years ago and with determination have transformed the place from a run of the mill public house into a superb country inn and restaurant. Much time and effort has also been put into the beautifully landscaped gardens. Inside the oak beamed ceilings and dominant walk - in fireplace lends itself to an evening of excellent food in the candlelit restaurant with friendly service.

The Harp Inn, Letterston 0348 840061 Map Ref: 3D

From Letterston,we took to the lanes on our journey northwards towards the countryside above Haverfordwest.Enjoying a beautiful countryside location on the **A487** between **St. Davids** and Haverfordwest at **Simpson Cross, The Victorian Conservatory Tea Room** provides a welcome stopping-off point in your journey through South Wales.

The Victorian Conservatory Tea Room, Simpson Cross
0437 710465 Map Ref: 4C

Monica and Peter are friendly hosts who have built up a deserved reputation for their superb clotted cream teas. The conservatory houses various tropical and exotic plants and fruit, including grapefruit, grapes and lemon balm geranium. From here you can admire the lovely surrounding countryside whilst savouring some of Monica's excellent home cooking. Weekends are always busy here, with Sunday roasts proving particularly popular, so please bookings only.

To the east we discovered a real find in the heart of the pretty village of **Wolfscastle, Wolfscastle Country Hotel and Restaurant.** This delightful establishment offers a taste of luxury with twenty beautifully furnished en-suite guest rooms, all equipped to the highest standards for maximum comfort. The hotel is renowned throughout the area for its excellent à la carte menu and bar lunches, all freshly prepared using the finest local produce, and not surprisingly, features in many guides including the prestigious 'Welsh Rarebit Hotels, The Gold Collection'. The bar provides a warm, welcoming atmosphere in which to enjoy a quiet drink or bar meal, and on fine days you can relax outside on the patio. For the energetic the hotel has a squash and tennis court and other leisure activities are readily available within a few miles of Wolfscastle.

Wolfscastle Country Hotel, Wolfscastle 0437 87225 Map Ref: 3D

We drove westwards through the tall hedged Pembrokeshire lanes back to the coast. We stopped at **Solva**, enchanted by its situation and the excellent craft shops on the road leading to the harbour. Solva harbour must be one of the most sheltered in Wales. It is at the end of a long inlet, well protected from the sometimes stormy waters of St Bride's Bay. Green hills roll down to the quayside, creating a picturesque scene. This was the last view of Wales for many 19th century emigrants, who sailed from Solva to America for 10 shillings,the price of a oneway ticket. In addition to its highquality craft shops, Solva is also the home of the Nectarium (don't look up the name in a dictionary for you won't find it there!). **The Nectarium** is a tropical butterfly farm, where colourful species from all over the world can be seen flying in a specially designed glasshouse

Situated in a secluded site at Lower House Skyfog,Solva **Min -yr-Afon** is holiday bungalow set in its own grounds. This well equipped three bedroomed holiday home is owned by Miss James, who provides

117

all except tea towels and towels. Those seeking to 'get away from it all' need look no further than Min -yr- Afon.

Min -yr- Afon, Lower House Skyfog, Solva Map Ref: 4B

In the heart of the Pembrokeshire Coast National Park with the Coastal Path literally running past the front door, **Harbour House Hotel** in Lower Solva is a super touring and holiday base.

Harbour House Hotel, Lower Solva 0437 721267 Map Ref: 4B

Here first class accommodation is provided in four attractively furnished, well-equipped guest rooms, three with en-suite facilities and the fourth with a separate bathroom nearby. The Anchor Bar offers a relaxing setting for a drink and provides a variety of entertainment for locals and visitors alike. The Fayre Clipper restaurant, as its name suggests, has a nautical theme, both in the decor and the extensive menu, but on Wednesdays the food has an international flavour when the menu features dishes from a chosen country, accompanied by appropriate wine and music.

Visitors to this delightful village will also discover an excellent stopping-off point at **The Cambrian**, a charming 17th century inn which can be found over the bridge on the Main Street, close to the river.

Friendly hosts Piero and Jean Cerri have built up a reputation for the varied menus they provide and in particular the excellent range of seafood, all available at very reasonable prices and accompanied by an extensive wine list. Food is available both lunchtime and evening and can be enjoyed in the warm, friendly atmosphere of the bar where you can choose from a selection of hand drawn ales, or alternatively on fine summer days, outside on the pleasant patio area.

118

Bishops Palace, St. Davids.

The Cambrian, Main Street, Lower Solva 0437 721210 Map Ref: 4B

Just one and a half miles North of Solva in the charming village of **Middle Mill** you can spend a fascinating hour or two at **The Woollen Mill**, where Robert and Cynthia Grime and their son Thomas produce wonderful carpets and floorcoverings to traditional and contemporary designs. The Mill has been in use since 1907 and still retains the original wheel. The whole weaving process, from the basic yarn to the finished product, is done on the premises, with Robert and Thomas doing the weaving and Cynthia in charge of the finishing process. You can watch weaving in progress during your visit and afterwards purchase a sample of the weavers' work in the adjacent Mill Shop.

The Woollen Mill at Solva, Middle Mill, Near Solva 0437 721597 Map Ref: 4B

Situated three miles from the coastal village of Solva on the road from **Croesgoch** to **Llandeloy, Lochmeyler Farm** is a delightful holiday base, surrounded by beautiful countryside. The delightful 16th century home of Morfydd Jones, it has been deservedly awarded the

Deluxe Grade for farmhouse accommodation and a four-crown rating by the Wales Tourist Board. Part of a 220-acre working dairy farm, the farmhouse itself has been sympathetically renovated and provides every modern comfort whilst retaining its original character. All the bedrooms are en-suite and offer full facilities, some with four-poster bed, and there is further accommodation of an equally high standard available in the newly converted Cottage Suites adjacent to the farmhouse. All meals are provided if required and are taken in the charming farmhouse dining room.

Lochmeyler Farm Guest House, Pen-y-Cwm 0348 837724 Map Ref: 4C

It was only a short drive to **St David's**, a tiny city - which must be the smallest in Britain - is named after Wales's patron saint. We were puzzled when we first arrived, for there appeared to be no sign of the cathedral, the building which gives St David's its city status. It was only after we parked the car near the centre and began to walk down the hill that the cathedral came into view. It is situated in a deep hollow well below the streets, so that not even its tall square tower is able to poke its way above the rooftops. We had to walk down the Thirty nine Steps at the approach to this ancient religious site before we could fully take in its magnificence. The cathedral, founded on the site of St David's 6th century monastic settlement, dates from the 12th century and contains many treasures. For us, the highlight of the interior was the oak roof, which displayed wonderfully ornate carvings by 15th century craftsmen. The cathedral has been an important Christian shrine since medieval times, when two pilgrimages to St David's equalled one to Rome. Successive monarchs from William the Conqueror to our present Queen Elizabeth have worshipped here. The Queen has a special seat reserved for her in the cathedral and recently distributed Maundy Money for the first time in Wales from St David's. The cathedral stands next door to another impressive religious site, the **Bishop's Palace**. Although now a roofless ruin, this 14thcentury palace would once have been the opulent residence of the influential leaders of the medieval church. For such a small place, we found so much to see.

Quite apart from the religious sites, there were pretty craft shops and attractions such as the Marine Life Centre.Visitors to this charming coastal town will soon discover the **The Farmers Arms** on Goat Street, a warm welcoming establishment run by Jim and Ronny Braby. The exterior still resembles the original row of cottages from which the pub was formed and inside, exposed stone walls and real log fires enhance the cosy atmosphere of the bars with in one small room numerous items of bygone memorabilia detailing the history of the town's lifeboats. You can choose from a wide selection of ales and tasty bar meals are served both lunchtime and evening. The patio is a real suntrap and one fine days provides a relaxing setting in which to enjoy your drink and meal.

The Farmers Arms, St. Davids 0437 720328 Map Ref: 4B

St Non's Hotel in St Davids is named after the saints mother and has much to offer. For those wanting that extra special touch, then the four deluxe rooms would be tempting. All have balconies and superb views to the coast and the stunning remains of the Bishops Palace. Alternatively, there are five guest rooms on the ground floor, all upholstered in Welsh tapestry,very warm and very much in keeping. All of the bedrooms are ensuite,centrally heated with clour televisions and tea/coffee making facilities. However, early morning tea breakfast and afternoon tea can be served to you in your room. With good service and a restaurant specialising in local seafood St Non's provides for all your needs during a stay in Britains smallest city.

St Non's Hotel, St. Davids 0437 720239 Map Ref: 4B

A short distance from the centre of St. Davids you will find a fabulous place to stay at **Warpool Court,** a magnificent old building steeped in history. It is particularly famous for the decorative antique tiles which tell the history of famous Welsh families.

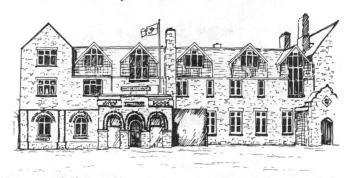

Warpool Court, St. Davids 0437 720300 Map Ref: 4B

The atmosphere here is warm and friendly and the hotel has a well-deserved reputation for its excellent cuisine and your friendly host, Rupert Duffin, goes out of his way to provide his guests with first class service and personal attention. Set within beautiful grounds offering lovely views across St.Bride's Bay, Warpool Court is a peaceful and relaxing haven from which to explore the many historic attractions of this lovely coastal corner of South West Wales. Facilities for swimming, tennis, golf, sauna, and croquet are also available.

Just along the road in a stunningly beautiful spot overlooking the sea is **St Non's Well,** next to the ruins of **St Non's Chapel.** Legend has it that David was born here during a great storm around AD500. The waters of St Non's Well are said to have magical powers for healing eye diseases, and were much visited by pilgrims to St David's. Another beautiful coastal spot close by, St Justinian's, is also steeped in legend. Justinian was a 6th century hermit who retreated across to **Ramsey Island** a short distance offshore to devote himself to God. A strict disciplinarian, he must have been too severe with his followers for they eventually rebelled and cut off his head. Justinian is then said to have walked across the waters of Ramsey Sound back to the mainland, carrying his head in his arms. The tiny little rockbound harbour named after him is now the location for the **St David's Lifeboat Station,** and also the place from which boat trips depart for Ramsey Island. Ramsey is a Norse name, a legacy of the Dark Age when this part of the coast was terrorised by Viking invaders.

Glan Y Mor, St. Davids 0437 721788 (Fax: 0437 721342) Map Ref: 4B

No such fear awaits at **Glan-Y-Mor** on Caerfai Road which is a welcoming guest house run by friendly hosts Clive and Cindy Pearce. Situated behind the Marine Life Centre, it is ideally situated as a touring base for this lovely area of South Wales and its many attractions. South facing, the bar looks out over St. Brides Bay and provides a relaxing setting for a quiet drink after a day's exploring. The guest rooms are attractively furnished and all have a washbasin and hot drinks facilities, whilst downstairs there is a residents' TV lounge complete with video. Each morning a wholesome cooked breakfast sets you up for the day and should you wish, a packed lunch is always readily available.

One of our favourite parts of Pembrokeshire came next on our travels. The north Pembrokeshire coastline between St David's and Cardigan is quieter than the more popular south. The places to stay here are small, while the rugged, rocky coastline consists of a succession of headlands, little bays and occasional sandy beaches. Our affection for this area goes back a long time, for as children we often holidayed in or near St David's.

Porthgain, has a sheltered harbour with a unique personality. The uniqueness comes from Porthgain's combination of natural beauty and industrial heritage. Dominating the harbourside is the shell of a 19th century brickworks, which stands close to remnants from Porthgain's heyday as a slate and graniteexporting port. We discovered,to our surprise,that many buildings in London and Liverpool are made from Porthgain granite. Nowadays, it's difficult to imagine the hectic scenes here 100 years ago when the harbour would have been packed with boats queuing for their cargoes of stone and brick needed for the building of the booming industrial towns of Britain. Porthgain's strange beauty has attracted many filmmakers.

Torbant Farm Guest House, Croesgoch 0348 831276 Map Ref: 3B

A little way inland from Porthgain is **Llanrhian**, and close by we were fortunate enough to find situated a mile east of **Croesgoch** on the A487 Fishguard to St. Davids road, **Torbant Farm Guest House** which offers excellent value accommodation and food. Dating back some 300 years, recent extensions have been made to carefully blend in with the age and character of the house, whilst providing every modern comfort. There are six attractively furnished guest rooms, three boasting en-suite facilities, and all with washbasins. The spacious dining room provides a relaxed setting for the day's meals and the adjoining lounge bar overlooks the excellent children's play area outside giving parents the chance to relax while their offspring play. It is only a mile and a half walk to the beautiful coastal scenery of North Pembrokeshire and its wealth of historic attractions, making Torbant Farm an excellent touring base.

If you are touring the area for the day and in need of some refreshment we suggested you stop off at **Trevine**. As you enter this ancient coastal village you will see the ruins of a grain mill, the demise of which inspired the well-known poem Melin Trefin by Archdruid Crwys. Whilst visiting this delightful village, call in at **The Ship** for a taste of traditional Welsh hospitality. Run by Jackie and Brian Maddocks, this charming inn is full of character with exposed stone walls, oak beams and a roaring log fire for those colder evenings. Here you can choose from a selection of fine hand-pumped ales and sample excellent homecooked meals, both in the bar and the restaurant. Look out for the lovely wall hangings which have been hand-woven by Jackie, a trained weaver, in her workshop just across the car park.

125

Pentre Ifan Burial Chamber.

The Ship, Trevine 0348 831445 Map Ref: 3C

Our time in Pembrokeshire was drawing to a close, and we were looking for something to take away with us as a memory of our stay. We followed the road to **Strumble Head**, a huge headland with a lighthouse built to warn ships of the cliffs on the approach to **Fishguard** harbour. **Carreg Wastad Point,** a remote headland near Strumble Head, was the scene of the last invasion of Britain. This farcical affair took place in 1797 when 1,400 French troops, led by an American colonel, attempted a halfbaked invasion which ended in surrender almost before it had begun. Memorabilia from the invasion can be seen at the Royal Oak Inn, which stands in the centre of Fishguard.

Fishguard's geography can be a little confusing. The old harbour a pretty little quayside is in Lower Fishguard, while the large modern harbour where the boats to and from Ireland dock is across the bay in Goodwick, just north of the town. We had heard stories of the good food in the town and just off the square in the main street, **Three Main Street,** appears at first glance to be a fairly ordinary Georgian town house.

Three Main Street, Fishguard 0348 874275 Map Ref: 2D

That is until you notice the blackboard outside with 'Dinner' and 'Accommodation' written in large letters. Once here you will soon realise you have discovered a 'hidden' gem, where the emphasis is on freshly prepared food, including locally caught fish, organically grown vegetables and even bread baked on the premises using organic flour. The lunch and dinner menus are both imaginative, mouthwatering and surprisingly reasonably priced with a fine accompanying wine list. To complete your visit, what could be nicer than staying overnight in one of the attractively decorated en-suite guest rooms.

Visitors will also find a super holiday base at the **Fishguard Bay Hotel** which stands surrounded by beautiful gardens and offering breathtaking views across the harbour and surrounding countryside. Steeped in history, the hotel was designated as a Building of Historic and Architectural Interest and has featured in two films during its varied and fascinating past. Today the discerning guest will find excellent cuisine in the hotel restaurant and first class accommodation ranging from very comfortable single rooms to luxury suites, all with excellent facilities and en-suite bathroom. The hotel radiates a quiet elegance throughout, with oak panelling and period furniture enhancing the relaxed atmosphere, ensuring a relaxing stay for the many visitors here.

The Pembrokeshire Coast National Park hugs the seashore for most of its length, venturing inland only to encompass the **Preseli Hills**. In the foothills of the Preselis is the **Gwaun Valley**, a place that really is hidden away. We wanted to visit this secluded, wooded valley for a number of reasons. Apart from its hidden qualities, we had been intrigued to discover that the locals still celebrate New Year on 13th January in keeping with the customs of the old pre 1752 calendar (which runs over a week and a half behind the times). We followed the **B4313** out of Fishguard to **Pontfaen** in the Gwaun Valley.

Fishguard Bay Hotel, Fishguard 0348 873571 Map Ref: 2D

There in the heart of the Pembrokeshire Coast National Park, **Tregynon Country Farmhouse Hotel** enjoys a unique position, perched on the edge of the spectacular Gwaun Valley. An attractive awardwinning 16th century farmhouse, it retains all its original charm with a beamed lounge featuring a large inglenook fireplace for you to toast your toes by in the cooler months. All guest bedrooms are centrally heated and provide colour television and hot drinks facilities, with en-suite shower/bathroom. Full breakfast is included. Renowned and imaginative, evening meals are available also catering readily for vegetarian preferences, using whenever possible the very best of local produce.

Tregynon Country Farmhouse Hotel, Gwaun Valley 0239 820531
(Fax: 0239 820808) Map Ref: 3E

Before leaving Pembrokeshire we took a drive through the Preseli Hills. Anyone interested in history will be fascinated by this haunting, treeless area of moor and mountain. The Preselis are scattered with prehistoric sites ranging from mysterious burial chambers to Iron Age hill forts. We followed the signs through the lanes inland from **Newport** to **Pentre Ifan Cromlech**, an ancient burial chamber with a huge 16ft capstone. It is made of the same Preseli bluestones that found their way somehow - no one has yet come up with a fully convincing explanation - to Stonehenge on Salisbury Plain.

Newport is a pretty little seaside centre with a fine beach. As its name suggests it was once an important port in the area before trade was diverted to Fishguard. It was also once the capital of the Marcher Lords of Cemaes, the only one not to have been abolished during Henry V111's reign. The remains of the 13th century Norman castle are now part of a mansion.

Finally we called in at **Dinas**, situated close to Dinas Head and island. The island is so called as it was, at the end of the Ice Age, separated from the mainland. The the church at **Cwm -yr- eglwys**

129

built in 1860 on the remains of one destroyed by a storm in 1839. The cove is considered one of the most attractive in Wales, enhanced by the virtual 500 foot cliffs of Dinas Head and a wonderful sight to remember as we moved on to our next destination.

CHAPTER FOUR

North - East Dyfed.

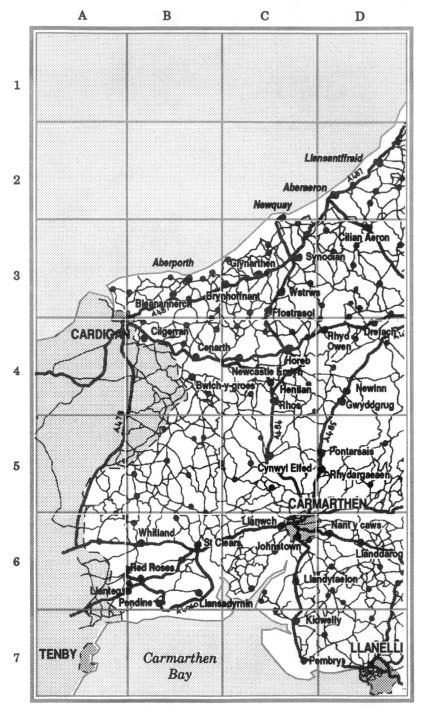

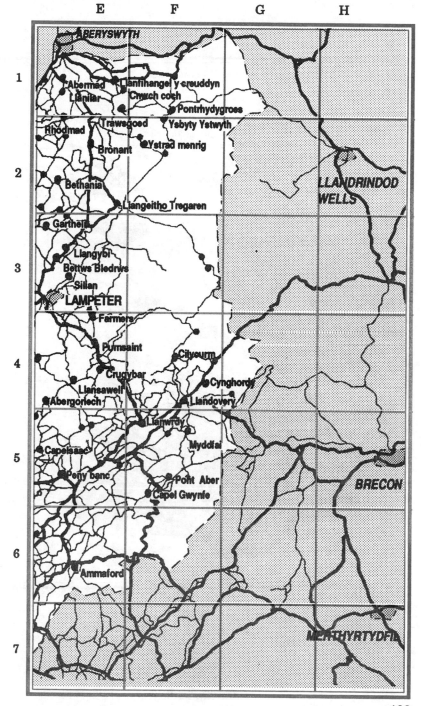

ABERYSWYTH

Abermad
Llanilar
Llanfihangel y creuddyn
Chwch coch
Pontrhydygroes

Rhodmad
Trawsgoed
Ysbyty Ystwyth
Bronant
Ystrad menrig

Bethania

Llangeitho Tregaren

Garthell

Llangybi
Bettws Bledrws
Silian
LAMPETER

LLANDRINDOD
WELLS

Farmers

Pumsaint

Cilyeurm

Crugybar
Cynghordy
Llansawell
Llandovery
Abergorlech

Llanwrdy

Myddfai

Capelsaac

Pony banc
Pont Aber
Capel Gwynfe

BRECON

Ammaford

MERTHYRTYDFIL

Cardigan Bay.

North - East Dyfed.

It isn't long before our travels through countryside splashed with colour and history took us towards **Cardigan** and into our next chapter. Our earlier preconceived impressions of South Wales had often misled us almost entirely, we'd learnt by now to keep our minds open and not to be surprised by what we came across and discovered. It proved to be, for us at least, a wise decision. From the small seaside towns that are dotted along **Cardigan Bays** beaches and bays to the rolling farmlands which rise to the **Cambrians** and eventually in the south east the **Black Mountains**, we were truly enchanted. Having just recently passed through the Pembrokeshire National Park, which is saturated in history as well as natural beauty, we thought that perhaps there'd be a respite. This was not the case as places of historical interest abound within an area that has a variety to please most visitors.

Before arriving at Cardigan we wandered around the back roads that lead from the National Park. In the pretty village of **Llantood**, one place well worth seeking out is **Croft Farm** which lies three miles south of Cardigan on the **A487** Fishguard Road. The farmhouse is over 100 years old and can be used for both bed and breakfast accommodation or as a self-contained luxury let, whilst within the grounds three converted farm buildings now house five superbly equipped self-catering cottages. Both the farmhouse and cottages carry the Wales Tourist Board 5 Dragon award for their first class facilities and in addition the farmhouse has the distinction of the Highly Commended grading and 2 Crown classification. Children are well-catered for with a comprehensive play area as well as a wide variety of animals to see and help feed. With essential supplies provided on your arrival and the added touch of a free bottle of wine and freshly cut flowers, Croft Farm is a very special 'hidden place'.

Close by we arrived at **Cilgerran** where the remains of **Cilgerran Castle** lie, sitting on a rocky premontory overlooking the river **Teifi**. The ruins have inspired artists such as Turner in the past and still continues to do so for todays painters. The castle is thought to have begun around 1093 but was strengthened by Gerald de Windsor who was granted it by Henry 1. Thereafter it changed hands many times,being partially sacked by Rhys ap Gruffyd in 1164, retaken by the Earl of Pembroke in 1204 before Llewelyn the Great captured it in 1233. Its final rebuild happened then but a hundred years later the castle was regarded as a ruin. However, the remains are inspiring and a visit is highly recommended. North of the village is **Cardigan Wildlife Park,** a fifty acre area of riverbank and woodland with nature trails,hides for observation and a picnic spot to tempt the visitor into this pleasant park.

Croft Farm, Llantood, Cardigan 0239 615179 Map Ref: 3A

Allt-y-Rheini Mansion Hotel, Cilgerran 0239 612286 Map Ref: 4B

As its name suggests, **Allt-y-Rheini Mansion Hotel** is a rather grand establishment and is a 'hidden place' where luxury and elegance combine in equal measure with a friendly, welcoming atmosphere. Lying in four and a half acres of lawned and wooded gardens it can be found by taking the Cilgerran turning at Rhos-hill from where it is signposted. Run by Chris, Chris and Enid, this magnificent 17th century mansion has five beautifully furnished en-suite guest rooms, a sunbed and steam bath to spoil yourself in, and a charming conservatory bar with panoramic views, which provides the perfect setting for a pre-dinner drink. Another bonus of staying here is the excellent homecooked food that Enid provides, all freshly prepared using the finest homegrown and local produce.

Attracted and intrigued by the name we headed across to **St.Dogmaels**. It was,gladly, nothing like we had envisioned. The remains of the 12th century Abbey founded by Robert Martyn for a Benedictine Order, on the site of the hermitage founded in the 6th century by St. Dogmael and then destroyed by Vikings, are modest. However,there are interesting carved and inscribed stones and within the Church on the site you can see the **Sagranus Stone**,inscribed in Latin and Ogham - the oldest written form of gaelic -which helped scholars in the 1840's interpret the Ogham alphabet.

We next visited **Cardigan**, its demise as a maritime port not diminishing the towns charm which is enhanced by the six arched Teifi Bridge spanning the river. The silting of the estuary along with the arrival of the railway was the main cause of Cardigans decline from a once busy port that had over three hundred ships registered there. The few remains of the castle, which fell to Parliament forces in 1645 and conceal a turbulent history, stand close by the river. Before that the castle had changed hands probably fifteen times during its use as the Welsh and English fought for supremacy in the area. On the river you might be fortunate enough to see fishing for trout being pursued from the traditional coracle. In the town,the Victorian guildhall is a noteworthy building where markets are often held that are sure to attract the curious visitor.

The surrounding coastline has many places of beauty and interest to visit,close by **Gwbert -on -Sea**,being no exception. The small resort on the Teifi's eastside is an excellent place for cliffwalks and surveying the estuary and its wildlife. Note should be taken of the times of tides should you choose the latter. Boat trips can be taken to round **Cardigan Island**,the home of seabirds such as terns,seals and wild Soay sheep.

One and a half miles away **Mwnt** is in National Trust land that compromises cliff,rocky headland and a beach that attracts many visitors. Mwnt was on the pilgrims route to Bardsey Island in the north - the saints burial ground. The Church of the Holy Cross, in a hollow originally to hide it from view and possible raids from the sea dates from the 15th century.

There are many places to stay and eat whilst in this area and for a tranquil rural base within easy reach of local attractions and sandy beaches, **Penrallt-y-Bie Farm** is ideal.

Situated on the **B4570** almost a mile from the village of **Ponthirwaun**, this beautiful farmhouse dates back to at least 1575 and friendly hosts, Keith and Miriam Davies have the original bill of sale written in Latin to prove it! Set within 189 acres Penrallt-y-Bie boasts a wealth of wild animal and plant life and there are many beautiful country walks close by. For the fishing enthusiast, use of a private half mile stretch on the River Teifi can be arranged at very reasonable rates. The farmhouse itself is full of character and there are four lovely guest rooms, each with colour TV, washbasin and hot drinks facilities.

Penrallt-y-Bie Farm, Ponthirwaun, Cardigan 023 987 388 Map Ref: 3A

One 'Hidden Place' where a memorable holiday is assured, is **Pen-Wern-Fach** in Pont-Hirwaun. Lying six miles up the River Teifi from Cardigan, this 18th century property was once the Home Farm for the famous Blaen-Pant Mansion Estate and boasts wonderful views of the Preseli mountains.

Pen-Wern-Fach, Pont-Hirwaun, Cardigan 0239 710694 Map Ref: 3A

Home of Hamish and Helen Cuthbertson, the farmhouse is now a

138

Welsh Tourist Board Two Crown guesthouse, whilst the original stone barns and stables have been beautifully converted into award-winning self-catering cottages. Each is named after a local river and although retaining original features such as oak beams and stone walls, every modern convenience is provided for maximum comfort. Guests are free to wander the six acres of grounds, home to a selection of friendly farm animals, and there is a large, safe play area, all of which makes this an ideal family holiday base.

Situated on the main **A487** at **Penparc** just a few miles from Cardigan, you will discover **Y Badell Aur Restaurant** which when translated, means 'A Pot of Gold' and that is exactly what it is. Tricia and Paul Davies are friendly, welcoming hosts who pride themselves on the superb food they prepare. Here in a relaxed, cosy atmosphere you can choose from an extensive menu with over 46 different dishes, as well as a separate vegetarian selection, giving guests a remarkable choice. Paul has been in catering for over 20 years and thanks to his skill, you can savour such delights as "Welsh Speciality", a terrine of lavabread, cockles and smoked bacon topped with Caerphilly cheese, followed by half a roast Ceredigion duckling with a rich orange and brandy sauce. The dessert menu offers far more than the average sweet trolley and to complete your meal you can enjoy a liqueur coffee. Having cooked your meal, Paul is likely to ask you personally whether everything was satisfactory, the answer to which is sure to be a resounding "Yes"!

Y Badell Aur, Penparc, Cardigan 0239 613610 Map Ref: 3A

A couple of miles away, **Penbontbren Farm Hotel** at **Glynarthen** is a truly out-of-this-world establishment which combines friendly, personal service with top class facilities. Travelling north from Cardigan on the A487 it can be found by taking the second right about one mile after Tanygroes (signposted Penbontbren). Owners Nan and Barrie Humphreys have created an award-winning holiday base here,

139

with accommodation, a restaurant and bar area, plus a countryside museum, all housed within beautifully converted farm buildings. The ten guest rooms are equipped to the highest standards, whilst the restaurant and bar area provides a charming setting in which to savour the excellent menu, including an extensive and imaginative vegetarian selection. The countryside museum houses a small collection of rural memorabilia and the farmland nature trail provides a delightful country walk.

Penbontbren Farm Hotel, Glynarthen 0239 810248 Map Ref: 3C

Meanwhile caravanners and camping enthusiasts would be well advised to veer off the beaten track and wend their way to **Pilbach Caravan Park** which is well-signposted off the **B4333 Aberporth** to **Newcastle Emlyn** road. Set within 15 acres of beautiful, gently sloping grounds, this is definitely a park as opposed to a campsite. The amenities here are first class and carry the highest accolade of five ticks from the Welsh Tourist Board. Facilities include a complete shower and toilet block, heated outdoor swimming pool, laundry room, large outdoor play area and a licensed club room and lounge where you can enjoy excellent bar meals. The small shop provides most essentials and a short drive will take you into Aberporth for further shopping. Pilbach Caravan Park, Bettws Ifan, Rhydlewis 0239 851434

The nearby **Aberporth,** once renowned for its herring industry is now a popular small resort for holidaymakers attracted by its location and sheltered sandy beaches. Set within forty two acres of beautiful, well-tended grounds with panoramic views over Cardigan Bay, **The Hotel Penrallt** at Aberporth is a simply fabulous holiday base, which blends luxurious accommodation with a homely, relaxed atmosphere. Boasting a 4-Crown Highly Commended rating, the hotel's sixteen en-suite guest rooms are all beautifully furnished and well-equipped, ensuring maximum comfort, whilst the complex of delightful self-catering cottages and apartments provide alternative accommodation of an equally high standard. The elegant panelled dining room is open to non-residents and provides an extensive and varied à la carte menu, catering to every taste. In the hotel's outstanding leisure complex you can choose to work off the holiday excesses or just relax and unwind, whilst some of Wales most beautiful countryside and historic places are just a short drive away.

Hotel Penrallt, Aberporth 0239 810227 (Fax: 0239 811375) Map Ref: 2D

Another place we would reccomend is **Ffynonwen** the delightful home of Peter and Olwen Duckworth who provide excellent overnight accommodation for visitors to Aberporth. To find this licensed guest house, take the Aberporth turning off the Cardigan to Aberystwyth road by the Gogerddan Arms and continue until you see Ffynonwen signposted on your left.

Ffynonwen, Aberporth, Cardigan 0239 810312 Map Ref: 3A

The house is about 300 years old and until 1972 was a working farm. Set within 20 acres of beautiful countryside it really does have

141

everything - a characterful bar area with adjoining verandah which proves a real suntrap, a comfortable guest lounge and seven well-equipped guest rooms, five en-suite, and one specially adapted for the disabled. All this, combined with first class hosts and fine homecooking, plus the use of two well-stocked pools of Rainbow Trout for fishing, make this an ideal holiday base.

Tresaith, only a few minutes away is another attractive, sheltered resort. The Afon Saith becomes a waterfall to the east of the village and the safe, shallow beaches that reveal golden sands and rock pools at low tide combine to attract families here. The village names literally means seven beaches but tradition has it that the name comes from seven princesses landing here after being cast away by their father.

If you take the Tresaith turning off the main A487 and follow the road to the beach, you will a quaint old-fashioned hostelry, **The Ship Inn**. This is a family-run freehouse, with owners, Bob and Tina Kentish sharing the workload with their two sons and daughter-in-law. Originally a single storey thatched building, The Ship was once a popular watering-hole for many a sailor transporting goods in and out of this beautiful cove. Today, refurbishment and extension has not detracted from its character and charm, and it provides a lovely setting in which to enjoy a refreshing drink and a tasty meal. For those wishing to stay, there are five lovely en-suite guest rooms, four with sea views and all with every modern facility for complete comfort.

The Ship Inn, Tresaith, Near Cardigan 0239 810 380. Map Ref: 3B

Standing proudly within five acres of magnificent grounds, **Glandwr Manor Hotel** in Tresaith offers a tranquil, rather luxurious base just five minutes walk from the sandy beach. Carrying a Three Crown Highly Commended rating by the Welsh Tourist Board, this Grade II listed Georgian building has been refurbished to very high standards by the current owners Janet and Arthur Davis and really is a credit to them, being grand from the outside, yet inside offering a warm and homely atmosphere. Exposed beams and open fires enhance the building's original character, whilst every modern facility is provided. Add to this the first class cuisine provided by the extensive restaurant menus and you really have all you need under one roof.

Glandwr Manor Hotel, Tresaith, Aberporth 0239 810197 Map Ref: 3B

We continued intending to wend our way along the coast but were soon lured into stopping at an **Penbryn** where the **Church of St. Michaels** overlooks a valley of woodland stretching down towards the large beach and sea. The church contains artefacts such as a weeping chancel and nearby remains have been uncovered of an Iron Age settlement. The shallow beach is ideal for beach days and the footpaths around offer pleasant walks.

Llangranog one of the most popular resorts in the area was our next destination. It lies in a narrow valley and reminded us of Cornish fishing villages. The surrounding headland and cliffs are National Trust Property and offer excellent walks and some rather dramatic scenery. Now you can only imagine the smuggling that once flourished in these parts. On the beach the story goes that the Devil having a toothache,pulled and then threw the tooth to land at the rocky crop known as **Carreg Bica.**

Off the main A487 Cardigan to Aberystwyth road, overlooking the sea at Llangrannog, **The Ship Inn** is a super stopping-off point. Run by two friendly couples, Kevin and De Brown and Lynn and Richard Box, it was built over 350 years ago and oozes character and olde worlde charm. Outside there is ample parking and a spacious seating area which regularly hosts events such as barbecues and pig roasts. Inside in a warm, relaxed atmosphere, you can choose from a fine selection of ales and a very extensive and varied menu. For those with exceptional appetites, you can try the Iced Seafood Platter subject to 24 hours notice, but you would be advised to fast for those 24 hours!

The Ship Inn, Llangrannog 0239 654423 Map Ref: 6D

Situated just fifty yards from the sea front in the village, adjacent to The Ship Inn, you will find a lovely place to stay at **Cilborth,** the charming home of Vicky and Mike Wright. This delightful house was formerly the inn outbuildings and is beautifully decorated throughout with pine furniture enhancing its character and charm. The kitchen has the unusual feature of lovely cupboards which have been handmade from wood that originally formed the platform at Aberystwyth station. The ground floor guest suite sleeps up to four and has additional facilities including washing machine, sink and cooker. Upstairs, a further guest room provides cosy accommodation for two and like the downstairs suite, has en-suite bathroom.

Cilborth, Llangrannog 0239 654681 Map Ref: 6D

Whilst in the village we also visited a relaxing haven at '**Frondolau Fach**'. This charming house has been so cleverly extended that you would think it had been standing here for many hundreds of years.

Within, there are four well-equipped and attractively furnished guest rooms, but outside to the rear you will find an acre of steeply climbing, carefully landscaped gardens which offer a breathtaking view when you reach the top. The house has its own parking area, which any visitor to Llangrannog will admit is a must, and it stands just 100 yards from the beach - what more could you ask for ?

Frondolau Fach, Llangrannog 0239 654748 Map Ref: 6D

Slightly inland at **Blaencwm Farm** situated on the **B4334** in **Brynhoffnant,** you will discover the perfect combination of comfortable accommodation in peaceful rural surroundings and a first class licensed restaurant. Set within ten acres of delightful landscaped gardens, complete with large, well-stocked lily ponds which form a haven for domestic and visiting wildfowl, it is ideal as a touring base. Within the farmhouse there are five attractively furnished guest rooms, two with en-suite facilities, whilst the former cowshed provides an olde worlde setting for the charming restaurant. Here you can savour a varied à la carte menu with both traditional and international dishes as well as a wide selection suitable for vegetarians.

Blaencwm Farm, Brynhoffnant 0239 654695 Map Ref: 3C

Cwmtydu is a secluded shingle beach and a public footpath from close by overlooks the coast and the chance to see seals or maybe even porpoises. For the more energetic **Cwmtydu Riding and Trekking Centre** is a 'hidden place' for horse lovers which can be found by turning off the main Aberystwyth to Cardigan road at the sign for Cwmtydu and after going through two crossroads, following the road round to the left towards the beach and the entrance is on the left.

Cwmtydu Riding and Trekking Centre. Pantrhyn, Cwmtydu
0545 56049 Map Ref: 2C

Originally started some 20 years ago with donkey rides on the beach, Cwmtydu is now a P.T.R.S.W. approved riding centre based in a 200 acre working farm, the home of Juliet and Raymond Rees. The one and two hour hacks cover some beautiful countryside and forestry land and the centre caters for every ability and can even offer rides for the disabled. Between Easter and October, visitors can choose to stay in Juliet and Raymond's 6-berth caravan which lies just 200 yards from the beach.

Situated in the village of **Llwyndafydd** just inland from Cwmtydu on our way to New Quay, **Ty-Hen Farm** is a working farm specialising in pedigree sheep. A rustic stone-built farmhouse dating from the 18th century, Ty-Hen also has seven self-catering cottages nestling in its rambling grounds. Roni and Mike Kelly are welcoming hosts who provide very comfortable bed and breakfast accommodation in five attractive guest rooms within the farmhouse, each with en-suite shower and offering lovely views of the surrounding farmland. Dining is a treat, with a superb four-course dinner provided each evening, complemented by a quality wine. The cottages are each individually named, character buildings all fully equipped and self-contained with oak beams enhancing the rustic feel. Guests are welcome to make use of the facilities in the main house and all guests can enjoy Ty-Hen's superb health and fitness centre which includes an indoor pool, multigym, sauna, steam room and solarium. With beautiful countryside on all sides and a children's area for younger members of the family, Ty-Hen has everything you need for the perfect family holiday.

Ty-Hen Farm, Llwyndafydd 0545 560346 Map Ref: 3C

It was a matter of miles to our next stopping off point, **New Quay**, a small, busy resort whose harbour now boasts more yachts than fishing boats. Like other harbour towns New Quays shipbuilding and coastal trading declined last century as road and rail links developed but the town retains a maritme charm. Its sands and boating facilities have long been an attraction for holidaymakers in search of a pleasant break. That being said there are many places in and around New Quay to detain the visitor and should you be inclined for food, drink or a place to stay, we suggest you try one of the places we visited.

The Seahorse Inn, New Quay 0545 560736 Map Ref: 2C

Situated in the heart of New Quay, **The Seahorse Inn** is a popular stopping-off point for visitors and locals alike. Believed to be 150 years old, it was originally called the Sailors Home Arms, later the Commercial Hotel and fifteen years ago was given the name Seahorse

147

Inn. Here you will find four spacious and well-furnished guest rooms all with shower, washbasin and every modern facility to ensure a comfortable stay. The bar provides a warm and welcoming atmosphere in which to enjoy a quiet drink and although no meals are served here, New Quay has a wealth of restaurants and eating houses to choose from.

Overlooking the harbour and sands, **The Hungry Trout** restaurant is renowned and well loved throughout this delightful area of South Wales. Built as a shipbuilders house in 1820, it later became a Post Office until the present owners, Ian and Margaret Hides bought it in 1980 and turned it into the super restaurant it is today. Inside the atmosphere is enhanced by beautifully laid tables and lovely furnishings. Ian's displays his culinary skill with an extensive and varied menu of both traditional and French cuisine as well as daily specials and a wide choice for vegetarians and children. Open both lunchtime and evening, the restaurant seats 40 and evening bookings are essential, to avoid disappointment.

The Hungry Trout, New Quay 0545 560680 Map Ref : 2C

The Black Lion Hotel is one of the oldest buildings in the small town, dating back to the late 17th century. Run by friendly hosts Kath and Tom Hunter, it is a wonderful hostelry, with eleven spacious and well-equipped guest rooms. The bar is traditionally furnished and full of character and there are wonderful views from the beer garden, which overlooks the sea and has a children's play area. However, the special feature here is 'Dylan's', the hotel restaurant named after Dylan Thomas who, during the 1940's was a regular visitor. Magnificent photographs and samples of his work adorn the walls for you to admire at your leisure while you sample some of the hotel's excellent homecooked fayre.

148

The Black Lion Hotel, New Quay 0545 560209 Map Ref : 2C

Just outside the resort for fine ale, excellent food and a first class atmosphere look no further than **Penrhiwgaled Arms** at **Cross Inn.** Turning off the main A487 onto the A486 New Quay Road, follow this road into Cross Inn and the Penrhiwgaled Arms is on your left. This mid-18th century inn was once a resting place for horses pulling carriages from New Quay, but today it is a delightful pub run by friendly hosts Sally and Tom Davies. There is ample off-road parking and a lovely beer garden, whilst inside a warm, welcoming atmosphere is enhanced by traditional beamed ceilings and a roaring log fire. With a wholesome menu accompanied by a selection of well-kept ales, this is a popular stopping-off point in any journey.

Penrhiwgaled Arms, Cross Inn 0545 560238 Map Ref : 3C

Meanwhile, camping enthusiasts will discover a truly outstanding holiday base at **Cei Bach Country Club** in **Parc-y-Brwcs**. To find this 'hidden' gem, take the **B4342** New Quay turning off the main

149

A487 and follow the road, turning right opposite the Cambrian Hotel from where it is signposted. Cei Bach carries the Welsh Tourist Board's 5-tick rating and has won the AA Environmental Award for Excellence in both 1991 and 1992, which gives some idea of the quality of facilities you can expect here. Set within six acres there are 60 pitches, 47 with electric hook-ups, and facilities for up to 40 tourers. In addition to the usual site amenities, there is a barbecue area and clubhouse which provides excellent bar and takeaway meals,whilst the games room and children's play area keep the younger visitors entertained.

Cei Bach, Parc-y-Brwcs, Ceibach 0545 580237 Map Ref : 3C

To the east of Newquay on the same road whether you prefer camping or self-catering chalets, **Bardsey View Holiday Park** in **Mydroilyn** caters for your every need.

Bardsey View Holiday Park, Mydroilyn 0545 580270 Map Ref : 3C

Taking the B4342 Mydroilyn road off the main A487, the park lies approximately two miles further up on the left. Set within five acres of landscaped grounds and offering lovely views of Cardigan Bay the site is immaculate. There are ten fully equipped chalet bungalows and facilities for ten tourers as well as 71 static caravans. The toilet block, laundry room and children's play area are all conveniently situated in the centre of the park and while the children enjoy the heated outdoor swimming pool, you can watch them from the comfort of the Country Club's lounge bar while you relax with a drink.

Roughly six miles further on up the coast the town of **Aberaeron** sits at the mouth of the Aeron Valley. Outside Aberaeron, situated on the main A487 at **Ffos-y-Ffin, The Red Lion** is delightful pub run by Graham and Rosh James who in the past two years have created a very friendly, welcoming establishment.

The Red Lion, Ffos-y-Ffin, Aberaeron 0545 570300 Map Ref : 2D

The attractive bar is full of character and the separate lounge area has the cosy intimacy of an old-fashioned front room. There is a wide selection of ales and the tasty homecooked food served both lunchtimes and evenings is a credit to the owners. The extensive blackboard menu changes regularly and offers excellent value, all dishes expertly prepared and served in portions substantial enough to satisfy the largest appetite. Outside, there is ample off-road parking and the side patio provides a pleasant setting in which to enjoy a drink on those warm Summer days.

From the town of Aberaeron, a pleasant walks can be taken by the river through woodland, that literally blooms at the right time of year. You can return by crossing Lover's Bridge and passing by a pond where the waterwheel stands that helped generate the power for the mill that now houses a craftworkshop. The town itself is quite delightful, with brightly painted Georgian style houses, especially around **Alban Square.** They are the result of town planning, which was initiated by local heiress Susannah Jones and took place during the 19th century. This influence was instrumental in turning the place from a small fishing hamlet into a busy port. The town was also famed for its shipbuilding, the schooners and sloops constructed by the harbour here once highly sought after. On the **Quay** there is a **Sea Aquarium** (Tel:- 0545 507142) which makes for an interesting visit and can be useful to know of on rainy days. The harbour itself can be crossed by the cable car **Aeron Express.**

The Hive on the Quay, Aberaeron 0545 570445 Map Ref : 2D

One place not to be missed whilst travelling through Aberaeron is **The Hive on the Quay**, where you can discover all there is to know about honey-bees and bumble-bees. The observation hives allow you to watch the bees at work and see how honey is produced which is reinforced by a fascinating video. The shop sells everything connected with bees, ranging from pure honey to Beeswax polish! Both the restaurant and the café serve superb food, often with a 'honey' influence, and the emphasis is always on freshly prepared, homemade fayre which includes locally caught fish and shellfish plus a variety of unusual salads. With the Sea Aquarium just along the quay and the Aeron Express running outside the gate, a fun family day out is assured.

To the rear of Aberaeron Sea Aquarium and overlooking the sea, **Pier Cottage** is one of the town's most historic buildings and makes a delightful touring base. Whether you decide to stay here for a night or two, or just call in to enjoy tasty homecooked refreshments in the tearooms, you won't be disappointed. Built circa 1812, Pier Cottage is the charming beamed home of Pat and Alan Bell who provide very comfortable accommodation in four lovely guest rooms, one of which is en-suite. Open from 10.30am - 6.00pm between Easter and the end of October, the tearooms serve a plentiful selection of homemade cakes, sandwiches, delicious milkshakes and tempting daily specials, which can be enjoyed in the courtyard, a real suntrap.

Aberaeron.

Pier Cottage, Aberaeron 0545 570132 Map Ref : 2D

Enjoying a central location on Market Street in Aberaeron, **The Monachty Arms Hotel** is a family-run establishment which combines a friendly pub atmosphere with full hotel facilities, making it an ideal holiday base for visitors to South Wales. The comfortably furnished Hotel Bar provides a relaxed atmosphere for a quiet drink whilst The Cellar Bar/Bistro offers a livelier alternative. The beer garden is perfect for warm Summer days and boasts wonderful views across the harbour. There are eight very tastefully decorated bedrooms, all equipped for maximum comfort and five with en-suite facilities. The 38-seater restaurant aims to cater for both simple and more adventurous tastes with its interesting menu or if you prefer, you can enjoy a light snack in the bar.

The Monachty Arms Hotel, Aberaeron 0545 570389 Map Ref : 2D

Aberarth can be easily neglected because of the charm of its more illustrious neighbour a mile away and the fact that the main road passes through it. However, make the opportunity to stop off at this small picturesque village. We were pleased to have made the effort to wander around as well as down on the attractive beach.

Continuing on our journey, we moved inland on the **B4457** through the small hamlets of Pennant, Cross Inn to a place that we had heard about and were curious to see. Situated at **Brynamlwg**, on the B4577, **Brimstone Wildlife Centre** is the brainchild of Chris and Marilyn Hurrell-Boydell and provides a superb family day out. With cascading waterfalls and a myriad of beautiful butterflies, plants and birds, the Tropical House gives you a taste of the Rainforest. At twice daily patting sessions children can meet a variety o f small animals and the parade of horses includes various breeds including the gentle Shire and the tiny Shetland pony. There is even pony trekking available for both the novice and more experienced rider.

The tea shop and licensed restaurant offers welcome refreshment with a wide selection of homemade food and in the evening, the restaurant becomes a bistro, recommended by the Good Food Guide for its mouthwatering and imaginative menu. Marilyn is an internationally renowned artist, famous for her pictures of butterflies and wild flowers, so before you leave, don't forget to pay a visit to the gift shop which houses a vast array of quality country gifts and samples of Marilyn's beautiful butterfly paintings and designs incorporated into aprons, tea towels and table cloths, all ideal mementos of an unforgettable day out.

Brimstone Wildlife Centre, Brynamlwg, Penuwch 0974 821439 Map Ref: 2E

The B4577 continues inland to meet the A485 which we followed in a northerly direction. We stopped at **Brynarth** in **Lledrod**, the delightful home of Brenda and Brian Ball who enjoy sharing the delights of their 17th century farmhouse with many guests throughout the year. The seven en-suite letting rooms are situated within the old outbuildings and have to be seen to be believed, providing every

155

modern facility whilst offering a peaceful and relaxing haven to stay in. Brenda and Brian also organise painting courses run by local professional artist Roy Marsden who provides comprehensive tuition in all aspects of painting and drawing techniques. With beautiful countryside surrounding Brynarth, there is a wealth of material for the artist to use and at the end of the day you can relax in front of the inglenook fireplace and enjoy a drink with your fellow guests.

Brynarth, Lledrod 09743 367 Map Ref : 1E

Back through rolling country to the coast where **Llannon** and **Llansantffraid** drew our attention. Peaceful hamlets with the latter on the coast, endorse the idyllic feel of the area. Signposted off the A487 in Llannon, you will find an excellent place to pause in your journey at **Plas Morfa Hotel and Restaurant**.

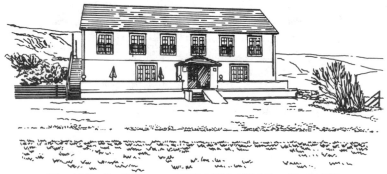

Plas Morfa, Llannon 0974 202415 Map Ref : 2D

Formerly a brewery and later a warehouse, this impressive building enjoys a peaceful location overlooking the sea and offers magnificent views in every direction. Full of character, the hotel has eight en-suite guest rooms, all well-equipped and beautifully decorated for maximum comfort. The ground floor restaurant provides a cosy, intimate setting for the exceptionally fine menu which is accompanied by an equally impressive wine list. For a livelier evening, you can venture "below stairs" to the bistro and bar in the former cellars where live entertainment proves a popular attraction with visitors and locals alike.

Further along by **Llanrhystud** evidence of ealier settlements in the area abound. To the south of the village,Castell Bach and Castell Mawr were once hillforts,seperated by a vale known as 'the dell of slaughter' in reference to an ancient battle. To the east the remains of the castle **Caer Penhros** overlook the village. Built around 1148 by Cadwaladr Ap Gruffydd,the castle was razed to the ground about fifty years later to avoid it falling into a rivals hands.

We finally entered **Aberystwyth** the largest town on Cardigan Bay,seat of local government and home to University College of Wales and the National Library of Wales. Although settlement in the area is known to have existed before, modern Aberystwyth can be traced to the castle,whose ruins still remain. Built in 1277 by Edward of Lancaster, it withstood a seige by the Welsh in 1294 and Owain Glyndwrs revolt in 1404 whilst the surrounding town was destroyed. For four years it served as a Glyndwr base. During the Civil War the castle was held for the royalist cause before surrendering in 1646.

The original buildings which were intended to be a hotel but eventually housed the beginnings of the University College stand opposite the castle ruins. The majority of the college lies to the east of town where you'll find the **Aberystwyth Arts Centre,** a well used venue for concerts,theatre productions and the **Catherine Lewis Gallery** with its permanent collection of art as well as constantly changing exhibitions. Close by the **National Library of Wales** holds many treasures of early Welsh and Celtic manuscripts. Among the many are the ' Black Book of Carmarthen ' dating from the 12th century, the oldest manuscript in Welsh. In the town the **Ceredigion Museum** tells of the history of Cardigan with an interesting collection of materials to illustrate their exhibitions. Look out for details of what is being held and when in the various establishments at the Tourist Information Offices (Tel:-0970 612125) close to the Museum.

The town itself is almost musuem like with the amount of well preserved 18th and 19th century buildings,especially around **Laura Place.** The seafront offers magnificent views of the whole of Cardigan Bay and the **Aberystwyth Electric Cliff Railway,**will take you to the top of Constitution Hill where even better views of the Bay can be had reaching from the Lleyn Peninsula in the north to Pembrokeshire in the south.

Aberystwyth.

Enjoying an enviable location on the promenade in Aberystwyth, **The Bay Hotel** is ideally located as a holiday and touring base. A family-run establishment, John and Hannah Davies and their two sons have been here for over twenty years and despite its size, the hotel still retains a friendly, personal touch. There are 31 guest rooms ranging from family suites to singles, all well-equipped and tastefully decorated, twenty-two with en-suite facilities. Two of them are situated on the ground floor making them suitable for the partially disabled. The spacious restaurant is open to non-residents and offers an extensive menu and after dinner, what better than to relax in the bar or entertainments room, where you can watch local performers.

The Bay Hotel, Aberystwyth 0970 61735 Map Ref : 1E

For railway enthusiasts a trip from the main station in town on the **Vale of Rheidol Light Railway** (Tel:- 0970 625819) will take you the twelve miles to **Devils Bridge** (more of this later in the chapter). The narrow guage line opened in 1902 to carry lead from the mines in the Rheidol Valley was soon taking passengers along this very attractive valley. British Rail operated it until 1988 when Brecon Railway acquired the line.

At **Llanbadarn Fawr** now a suburb of Aberystwyth but once the early pre - castle town the Church was a 6th century bishopric founded by St. Padarn, later in the 8th century merging with St. David. The present building is of 13th century origin and contains the tomb of St. Padarn and two Celtic crosses that are associated with St. Samson the brother of Padarn.

Not far from Aberystwyth on the A487 is a turn off for the village of **Borth.** We thought that it sounded rather like a name from a story book. It was here that we came to visit a very unusual establishment called **Borth Animalarium.** The Animalarium is the dream of a the Crowthers. Their idea was to turn a hobby of showing rabbits and poultry into a business. Ann had managed the children's farmyard at the National Agricultural Centre at Stoneleigh in Warwickshire for two years and thought they could make a more interesting exhibition themselves.

Borth Animalarium, Borth 0970 871224 Map Ref : 1E

Starting with a bare field they gradually built up the collection of animals. There are goats,rabbits,raccoons,lemurs,monkies and many more. A creepy crawly section displays stick insects,scorpions and tarantulas. There are lizards,snakes and terrapins in the reptile house as well as a variety of tortoises and exotic birds. All the animals thrive in this impressively run establishment. If you talk to the Crowthers you will find their enthusiasm, affection and pride for the Animalarium infectious. There is a souvenir shop for mementoes of your visit, snacks and drinks are also available. The whole area is quite flat and there are ramps for disabled access where necessary. Most displays are under cover which combine to make a visit,even on wet days, pleasant and comfortable.

We then followed the **A44** out of Aberystwyth on the north side of the Rheidol Valley to **Ponterwyd**. There's a pub here called Borrow Arms,recalling that the linguist George Borrow -who once worked for the British and Foreign Bible Society and wrote a book on gypsies - dried out after staggering through a peat bog.

Originally a Coaching Inn over 400 years old, **Dyffryn Castell** in Ponterwyd is now a welcoming, family-run hotel providing a comfortable holiday base from which to discover the beauty of South Wales. Friendly proprietors Islwyn and Angharad Jones have created a first class hotel and restaurant. The hotel has nine well-furnished guest rooms and downstairs, make sure you look out for the feature fireplace in the bar area where a child's shoe is displayed which was discovered in the old fireplace 150 years ago.The attractive dining room offers an extensive menu or if prefer, you can choose from a wide selection of bar snacks and the beer garden, complete with play area, is the ideal setting for a quiet drink .

Dyffryn Castell Hotel, Ponterwyd 097085 237 Map Ref : 1F

We joined the **A4120** for the short trip to **Devils Bridge**, the destination of the Rheidol Railway. This beauty spot attracts many who come to view the waterfalls drop 300 feet as the river changes direction from south to west. An iron bridge built in 1901 straddles the top of the falls and just below it there is a stone bridge from 1753. Further down still lies the original Pont -y-gwr-Drwg(Bridge of the Devil). The bridge is thought to have been built by monks from the **Strata Florida Abbey** which lies eight miles south.

There are many footpaths to follow for different vantage points, the Forestry Commission have trails and picnic sites at the **Arch.** The arch was erected by Thomas Johnes in 1810 to honour the Golden Jubilee of George 111. He also transformed the area with forestation, planting the area with over four million trees as if in anticipation of the Forestry Commission.

Situated on the A4120 at **Pisgah,** half way between Devils Bridge and Aberystwyth, the aptly named **Halfway Inn** is a superb example of a traditional hostelry. Set 700 feet above sea level with breathtaking views across the Rheidol Valley, this delightful freehouse is run by welcoming hosts Ray Wood and Sally Roger. The inn dates back several hundred years and an atmosphere of olde worlde charm is enhanced by thick stone walls, flagstone floors and open log fires for those chillier days. Internationally renowned for its range of Real Ales, in the Stone Room you can pour yourself a pint straight from the cask. As for food, the quality and choice here is far and above standard 'pub fare', ranging from freshly made sandwiches and popular grills to an extensive selection of specialities. Finally, what could be nicer than to retire to one of the two beautifully furnished, en-suite guest

Devils Bridge.

rooms, which are equipped with every modern convenience to ensure maximum comfort.

The Halfway Inn, Pisgah 0970 84 631 Map Ref : 1E

From Devil's Bridge we wound our way south on the **B4343** through **Pont-rhyd-y-groes** to **Pontrhydfendigaid-Bridge** near the ford of the Blessed Virgin - where a mile and a half to south east lies the ruins of Strata Florida Abbey. This Cistercian abbey in the ' Plain of Flowers ' was founded in 1164 only to have its lands overrun by Rhys ap Gruffyd two years later. In 1184 he refounded the Abbey and most of the ruins date from this period onwards. During the 12th and 13th centuries the Abbey acted as the political and religious centre for Wales - in 1238 Welsh princes swore their allegiance to Llewelyn the Greats son Dafydd in the Abbey. It also flourished in terms of wealth during this period, mainly through wool from the sheep that grazed on its vast lands which spread as far as Rhayader in the east. After Dissolution, the land passed through various hands and is now in the hands of CADW. (Welsh Historic Monuments)

The ruins consist mainly of the cloister and chapter house by the church which today serves the parish of Pontryhydfendigaid. Inside there are remains that have been integrated into the church and in the north transept stands a memorial to Dafydd ap Gwilym, considered by some to have been one of the greatest Welsh poets in the 14th century. His remains are thought to be buried here or at Talley.

A pleasant walk can be made beyond the Abbey in a north easterly direction to Llyn Teifi - small lakes that are the source of the river Teifi. The two and a half miles can be followed by paths to a contrasting countryside from that around the abbey.

Leaving this attractive location and following the B4343 we came to **Cors Caron Nature Reserve** an almost 2000 acre reserve which contains the largest peat bog in Wales. With the river Teifi running through it, the reserve attracts the interest of botanists and

163

Strata Florida Abbey.

ornithologists alike for obvious reasons. You can view this interesting landscape for yourself from a disused embankment which had parking facilities.

Four miles further down the road you'll arrive at **Tregaron,** a small market town that serves the surrounding area. Here you'll have the opportunity to again observe the life of a market town,especially if you are there on Tuesdays when the market is on and farmers,traders and livestock are in town. In the square there is a statue of Henry Richard the liberal MP and son of Tregaron, a vociferous supporter disarmament and sometimes known as the 'Apostle of Peace'.

Llanddewi Brefi also on the same road was host to a synod in 519 which St.David attended. They were debating the Pelagian heresy, a doctrine that advocated freedom of thought rather than the biblical version of original sin that determined the morality of the time. St.Davids Church in the village stands on a mound which tradition says rose as St.David preached during the synod. The church itself dates from the 13th century and inside contains some old inscribed stones. One known as St.Davids Staff and another with an Ogham inscription that has been suggested commemorated a heretic of the sort that St.David was denouncing.

The road passes by the sites of several hillforts including **Llanfair Clydogau,** where the Romans mined for silver, sits by the Sarn Helen - a military road. The road once connected a gold mine in the south at Dolaucothi and a fort at Bremia in the north.

Lampeter, has long been the centre for this part of the Teifi Valley but is perhaps best known for **St.David's College.** It is the oldest degree institution in Wales having been founded in 1822 by Bishop Thomas Burgess of St.Davids. Since 1971 integrated with the University of Wales the campus however still retains its original atmosphere.The town itself has a pleasant mixture of Victorian and Georgian buildings with choices of places to eat or stay.

In the centre of the market town of Lampeter, you will find an impressive family-run 17th century coaching inn, **The Black Lion Royal Hotel.** This Grade I listed building is probably the oldest in Lampeter and to the rear of the hotel, the old stables and drivers accommodation still stand, mementos of its coaching past. The interior is traditionally furnished in keeping with the character of the building and there are fifteen superbly equipped bedrooms, each with en-suite bath or shower and one boasting a whirlpool bath. There is a wide selection of bar meals available and the restaurant offers an extensive and varied menu which has something to please every palate. During your stay, don't forget to look out for the resident lady ghost!

The Black Lion Royal Hotel, Lampeter 0570 422172 Map Ref : 3D

Situated on the High Street, **The Castle Hotel** has been offering travellers accommodation and refreshment for over 200 years. Full of character, the hotel is cosy and inviting, a place where you can call in and sample a welcome pint of traditional ale or savour a tasty, homecooked meal. Food is served every lunchtime and also on Saturday evenings, with a menu which is both extensive and varied, to suit every palate. Families are welcome and should you wish to stay, there are five tastefully decorated guest rooms offering very comfortable overnight accommodation. Please note, the hotel bar and restaurant is closed on Sunday evenings.

The Castle Hotel, Lampeter 0570 422554 Map Ref : 3A

A few miles to the west of you'll find **Ystrad Aeron** a pleasant country village lying midway between Aberaeron and Lampeter and it is here, situated on the **A482,** that you will find the **Vale of Aeron**, a traditional Welsh inn dating back to the 17th century.

Vale of Aeron, Ystrad Aeron, Felinfach 0570 470385 Map Ref : 3D

Currently owned by friendly hosts Daphne and Rowland Evans, this delightful establishment has been run by members of Daphne's family since the turn of the century and is a place full of character, with beamed ceilings, exposed brickwork and many old farm tools adorning the walls. Here in a warm, welcoming atmosphere you can sample a fine selection of ales and savour excellent homecooked food from an extensive lunchtime and dinner menu, making this an ideal place to break your journey.

Minutes walk from the centre of historic Lampeter the Castle Green Inn offers a warm welcome, fine ales and good food; Bryan and Mavis Benyon are the hosts.

The Castle Green, Bryn Road, Lampeter 0570-422348 Map Ref : 3A

Bryan has been a chef for many years at top hotels and the menu selection reflects this. Pheasant in black cherry sauce and sirloin with oysters in mushroom and brandy sauce are just two of the choices.

The Castle Green Inn has also been re-furbished recently. There is an open fire and comfy seating in the bar, the lounge is both pretty and cosy, and should you wish to stay there are five comfortable en-suite rooms.

We took the **A475** from Lampeter and turned onto the **B4337** and soon found a pleasant place to stop. Enjoying a pleasant rural location in the centre of **Drefach** village in the Teifi Valley, **The Sandpiper** combines a super licensed restaurant with good overnight accommodation.

The Sandpiper, Drefach, Llanybydder 0570 480249 Map Ref :4D

Your welcoming hosts here are Paul and Heather Longley and Dave Archer, the restaurant chef, and their combined hard efforts have transformed this 100 year old building and created superb surroundings in which to savour the extensive restaurant menu or relax in the lounge bar with a drink. Open from 9.00am until late evening, you can enjoy any meal of the day here, and after dinner, what could be nicer than retiring to one of the five very comfortable guest rooms, all attractively furnished and well-equipped, two with en-suite bathrooms.

Y Gwrdy Mawr Inn, Llanybydder 0570 480210Map Ref :4D

We'd heard of the horse fairs that are regularly held at **Llanybydder** but were unfortunate enough to arrive at the wrong time. However,there are several woollen mills to visit in this centre of weaving. We also discovered situated on the outskirts of Llanybydder village on the A485 a lovely place to stop at **Y Gwrdy Mawr Inn**.

Built some 300 years ago, the inn has served many purposes over the years, including providing accommodation for nuns and at one time being a mortuary, until it later became an inn. Split into three sections, there is an open front bar area, a cosy central bar and a rear restaurant section which leads onto the lovely patio, a real suntrap during the warm Summer months. Open all day, this traditional inn serves a selection of fine ales and homecooked meals and provides a welcome break as you journey through this lovely area of South Wales.

As we drew closer to **Llandyssul** we were drawn to an attractive place standing in five acres of magnificent grounds with nature trails, ponds and a wealth of other natural treasures, **Waunifor.** It's a small country estate in the village of **Maesycrugiau** which provides first class self-catering accommodation. Awarded a Welsh Tourist Board Dragon Grade 3 rating, the facilities here ensure a happy and relaxing holiday for all, with ten fully equipped letting units each with their own distinctive character. Additional facilities include a covered, heated swimming pool, a tennis court and in the ground floor of the main house, a games room, small library and a payphone. Babysitting services can be provided if required and large group or special interest holidays can also be catered for here, making Waunifor a complete holiday centre.

Waunifor, Maesycrugiau 0559 35280 / 430Map Ref :4D

Perhaps two miles away and recently listed by the CADW as an historical place of interest, **Rock-Mills** water mill in **Capel Dewi** was built back in 1890 by the great grandfather of Donald Morgan, the present owner, and has always been family-run. Enjoying a delightful setting beside the River Clettwr, the mill boasts an unusually large waterwheel which is twice the width of most. Many items such as blankets and table linen are still produced here and you can see part of the production line in progress when you visit, although a full display details all the various process involved. After discovering how the fabrics are made you have the opportunity to purchase some of the mill goods and other locally produced crafts in the mill's shop. Situated on the **B4459** at Capel Dewi, just off the A475 at **Rhydowen** or off the A485 at **Alltwalis**, Rock-Mills is open from 9.00am - 5.30pm Monday to Friday (Jan-Dec) and Saturday 9.00am - 1.00pm (May-Sept only).

Rock-Mills, Capel Dewi, Llandysul 0559 362356 Map Ref : 4C

The town of Llandyssul is another centre for the wool industry, **Maesllyn** (Tel:- 0239 75 251) being a working museum and one of many you can visit It is also the birthplace of Christmas Evans a Baptist minister in the early 19th century who was famed for his fiery,emotional sermons. Becoming a Baptist because his ideal choice,the Presbyterians, demanded academic standards he hadn't achieved; he preached mainly in the Lleyn and Anglesey.

There are many 'idyll's' hidden away in the surrounding delightful countryside and we discovered several worth more than just mentioning. It is hard to know where to begin describing what **Pengraigwen** has to offer the holidaymaker, but since 1988 when it was an old run-down farmhouse, it has been completely refurbished by the present owners, Beverley and John Michael and is now the sort of place most people would like as their home. Whether you decide to take a riding holiday, a painting holiday or a photographic holiday, you will find the facilities here outstanding. There is superb accommodation provided in four comfortable en-suite guest rooms, situated in the converted barn and mealtimes, a major feature of every holiday, are enjoyed en masse at the large refectory dining table within the farmhouse. The property has an art gallery, and bed and breakfast is also available.

Pengraigwen, Llandysul 0559 362305 Map Ref :4C

In a south easterly direction from Llandyssul, situated approximately one mile off the **B4459** at **Pencader** and 750 feet up on the crest of a hill, **Arlandir** is the lovely home of Jackie and Alan Wonfor. Starting quite literally from scratch, it has taken them three years to build this super bungalow which enjoys a beautiful setting in outstanding gardens with magnificent views of the surrounding countryside. There are two attractively furnished and well-equipped guest rooms which are suitable for the partially disabled, one with en-suite shower and one with private bathroom adjacent. Children and pets are welcome and in addition to a full breakfast, you can enjoy Jackie's fine Welsh cooking in the evening, by prior arrangement.

Arlandir, Pencader 0559 384872 Map Ref :4C

Pellorwel when translated, means 'Far Horizons', and this is the apt name given to the charming home of Joan and Michael Austwick, tremendous hosts who provided first class bed and breakfast accommodation. Ideal as a holiday or touring base, Pellorwel can be found by following the A486 north from Llandysul and passing through the crossroads at Horeb and Croeslan. The house stands on the lefthand side about 100 yards through the crossroads at Bwlch-y-groes. A picture both inside and out, Pellorwel is set within a garden as pretty and ornate as Ann Hathaway's, with various homegrown vegetables providing the ingredients for Joan's excellent homecooking. All the rooms are spacious and well-decorated with all the furniture made by Michael, who is clearly a real craftsman.

Pellorwel, Bwlch-y-groes 0239 851226 Map Ref :4B

In the same area and for a peaceful holiday base surrounded by some of Wales' most beautiful scenery, **Broniwan**, a charming 19th century working farm, is ideal. Run by Carole and Allen Jacobs here you will find first class bed and breakfast accommodation.

Broniwan, Rhydlewis 0239 851261 Map Ref :4C

Enjoying a hillside setting, overlooking the village of Rhydlewis, this is an immaculate and attractively furnished house featuring the original pitchpine staircase and panelling, with accommodation including ensuite in three lovely guest rooms. Superb cuisine is provided both at breakfast and in the evening, creatively prepared using much of the organic farm produce. It comes as no surprise, therefore, to learn that Broniwan has been awarded the Farmhouse Award and a 2-Crown Highly Commended rating by the Welsh Tourist Board.

We returned on the B4334 with the intention of going to **Newcastle Emlyn** via **Henllan** where we thought we'd enjoy another of Wales narrow gauge railways. The river Teifi meanders through some of the most spectacular scenery of South Wales and what better way to see it than from **Teifi Valley Railway.** You don't have to be a railway enthusiast to appreciate this super tourist attraction, but you probably will be after being hauled by steam and diesel locomotives through the breathtaking Teifi Valley countryside. Your journey begins and ends at the railway headquarters in Henllan village and from the platform here you can follow a delightful woodland walk with a nature trail providing a wealth of animal, plant and birdlife. Further into the woods in a quiet glade there are picnic tables for visitors use, but if you forget to bring your own provisions, refreshments are available in the Railway Tearoom.

The Teifi Valley Railway, Henllan 0559 371077 Map Ref :4C

To the south in **Drefach Felindre** the **Musuem of the Welsh Woollen Industry** stands as homage to the important role this textile played in the economy and well being of the area. The museum, a branch of the National Museum of Wales, recalls the past through exhibition and a collection of tools, machinery and demonstrations (Tel:- 0559 370929).

The castle remains at Newcastle Emlyn are little beyond a gateway. Like other castles in Wales, its turbulent history is in someways confirmed by it present condition. Changing hands several times until it was destroyed during the Glyndwr rebellion in the early 1400's the castle fell into disrepair until given to Sir Rhys ap Thomas by Henry V11 in the 16th century. The castle was destroyed after the Civil War for Royalist sympathies. The town is a modest but attractive place and the home to the first printing press in Wales, set up by Isaac Carter in 1718.

In the centre of Newcastle Emlyn on Sycamore Street, you will find **Casa Nostra,** a wonderful restaurant which caters for absolutely everyone. Tastefully decorated throughout, with attractive plate displays on the walls and beautifully laid tables, the cosy and intimate atmosphere is enhanced by dim lighting. Open daily from 9.00am until 10.30pm, the menu ranges from a full breakfast and light snacks, to hot and cold lunches and a mouthwatering selection of dishes for dinner, with a fine accompanying wine list. Friendly chef/proprietor Eduardo Pereira has had many years experience in catering and in addition to Casa Nostra also owns The Pensarnau Arms in nearby Pentrecagal, both establishments attracting a large local following.

Casa Nostra, Newcastle Emlyn 0239 71007 Map Ref : 4C

Situated on Station Road at Newcastle Emlyn, **The Coopers Arms** proves a popular stopping-off point with holidaymakers. This delightful 100 year old inn is run by a friendly couple, David and Christina Taylor who offer the thirsty traveller a welcome selection of beers, lagers and Real Ales. If you are feeling hungry you can choose to sample one of the specials at the tile-topped bar, or alternatively make a real meal of it and enjoy three courses in the attractive surroundings of the restaurant which adjoins the bar through a stone archway. If you are a non-smoker, there is a separate non-smoking dining area. You can even take it outside in the beer garden while the children enjoy the play area, but whatever you choose, the food is sure to be excellent since Christina is a first class cook.

Coopers Arm, Newcastle Emlyn 0239 710323

Situated on the **A484** road to **Cenarth** just one mile out of Newcastle Emlyn, **Maes-y-Derw** is an impressive Victorian house standing proudly on the hillside. Home of Diane and Wyn Davies, this is a simply delightful holiday base set in eleven acres, with a further 30 acres of meadowland adjacent to the River Teifi, for which the house holds two fishing permits. Originally built by a carpenter, examples of his craft are evident throughout the house. The three guest bedrooms are all beautifully furnished and have either private or en-suite bathroom. Alternatively, the holiday cottage which adjoins the house, provides self catering accommodation of an equally high standard. Maes-y-Derw has a residential licence and Diane is happy to provide evening meals if required.

Maes-y-Derw, Newcastle Emlyn 0239 710860 Map Ref :4C

Whilst in the area we made an interesting visit to **Felin Geri Mill** near **Cwm Cou** where a 17th century working watermill is open to the public (Tel:- 0239 7108100). Here you can watch the various stages of grinding flour as well as take the opportunity to purchase their produce.

The A484 more or less follows the river Teifi and we soon came to Cenarth, a place which attracts many visitors throughout the year. The Fall are an attraction in themselves but so is the hope of viewing Coracle men trying to catch salmon from the river below. The use of the craft is fast disappearing and for an informative visit **The National Coracle Centre** in Cenarth Falls that is well worth visiting. Lying adjacent to Cenarth Mill, this first class "museum" which stands on the site of the mill's former pig stys and workshops, portrays the fascinating history of the coracle through clearly laid out displays with exhibits from all over the world. Thanks to the hard work of Martin Fowler and his wife, the public can now follow the story of this unique craft, from the first civilisations to the present day, where it is still used, both for fishing and as an unusual and peaceful form of transport. Within the centre there is also a wonderful craftshop where you can browse before choosing a memento of your visit to this very special place.

The National Coracle Centre, Cenarth Falls 0239 710980 Map Ref :4G

There are a variety of places here which we recommend should you wish to use the attractive area as a base for your visit. On the main A484 Cardigan to Newcastle Emlyn road at the edge of Cenarth village, non-smokers will discover a relaxing haven at **Y Garreg Lwyd.**

Y Garreg Lwyd, Cenarth 0239 71023 Map Ref : 4B

Its name means 'The Grey Stone' and such a stone was fairly recently unearthed within the grounds. Home of Helen and Jerry Daly, this 18th century house has quite a history, having at one time been a mason's house and later a small farm forming part of the Cawdor Estate. It was also the birthplace in 1852, of William Eilir

Evans, a cleric, poet and journalist of some repute. Today though, it is a beautifully furnished and very comfortable holiday base, with two lovely letting rooms and a delightful dining room which was once a cowshed!

On the left as you enter the village you will find a superb holiday base at **Cenarth Falls Holiday Park.** The facilities here are commensurate with the 5-tick 'Excellent' grading awarded the park by the Wales Tourist Board. Here you stay in a spacious and luxurious Dragon Award caravan, offering first class amenities including colour television, microwave, fridge/freezer and full size cooker. Park leisure facilities are excellent, with a licensed clubhouse which serves evening bar meals, a heated outdoor swimming pool, games room, children's play area, shop and launderette. With all this you hardly need to leave the park, yet with the River Teifi nearby, beautiful walks abound and for the fishing enthusiast, the park has use of a private stretch of river.

Cenarth Falls Holiday Park, Cenarth 0239 710345
Map Ref : 4B

In the centre of Cenarth adjacent to Cenarth Falls on the Cardigan to Newcastle Emlyn road stands a delightful pub called **The Three Horseshoes.** Formerly described as Cenarth's 'Alehouse by the church' in 1760, this charming ivy-clad building provides only real ales. Sympathetically refurbished by present owners Russ and Glenys Tustin, it still retains various original features including the interior roof, brew pot, chimney and thatch. The interior is attractively decorated with prints and bygone memorabilia and awards won by Russ in earlier days when he played with Swansea as prop forward. With a superb, menu featuring plenty of local produce, and a delightful outdoor garden area offering lovely views over Cenarth Falls, this is an establishment not to be missed.

177

The Three Horseshoes, Cenarth 0239 710119 Map Ref: 4B

Whilst at Cenarth Falls you can take a step back in time when you visit **The Old Smithy Craftshop and Heritage Centre,** a unique museum enjoying an idyllic location within the sound of the famous Salmon Leap Falls.

The Old Smithy Craftshop and Heritage Centre, Cenarth Falls
0239 710067 Map Ref: 4B

Run by a charming couple, Barbara and Graham Elliott, their hard work and determined efforts have turned this 18th century forge into a superb museum and today you can see a vast array of original smithy equipment and other rural bygones, of the area. As you pass through the exhibition you will find yourself in one of the best stocked gifts shops anywhere, with all kinds of arts, crafts and knick-knacks beautifully displayed providing an array of tempting mementos. There is also ample parking and a picnic area within the grounds.

At **Llechryd** you'll discover that the church there is known as the

Coracles on the river.

Coracle Church and set in the heart of the village on the main A484 Cardigan to Newcastle Emlyn road, **The Carpenters Arms** is a delightful Welsh inn with a lively, welcoming atmosphere. Over 100 years old, it has always been an inn and was once part of the Fisherman's Arms when beer was brewed in the cellar. Today you can sample fine ale and excellent food, with an extensive menu providing a wide selection including children's meals. For visitors wishing to stay, The Carpenters has four very comfortable letting rooms, one with en-suite bathroom. Friendly hosts John and Barbara Potts also have a six-berth caravan in the grounds which is available throughout the season and a five-bedroomed bungalow near Crymych which is open all year round and sleeps ten.

The Carpenters Arms, Llechryd 0239 87692 Map Ref : 4B

We doubled back upon ourselves on minor roads and found in the peaceful village of **Abercych** on the **B4332** a mile from Cenarth, a delightful country pub **The Penrhiw Inn**.

The Penrhiw Inn, Abercych 0239 87229 Map Ref : 4B

Bob and Ros Purnell are friendly hosts who offer the best of everything, whether it be food, ale or accommodation. Outside there is ample parking space and to the rear, the views of the Teifi Valley are simply breathtaking. Inside, the bar is full of character, with exposed stone walls adorned with a variety of motoring memorabilia. The wide range of ales includes Buckley's Bitter and drinks can be accompanied by a tasty basket meal. With four attractive guest rooms providing very comfortable accommodation all year round, The Penrhiw Inn seems to provide everything you need.

Continuing on the back roads through delightful country to a secret and unspoilt gem, **Morlogws,** off the **B4333** near **Capel Iwan,** a working farm set in 160 acres, where a holiday to remember is assured. Here Mair, Haydn and Aled Jones offer a warm Welsh welcome and provide a taste of Wales at its best, whilst making you feel completely at home.

Morlogws, Capel Iwan, Newcastle Emlyn 0559 370282 Map Ref : 4B

Haydn is the fifth generation to farm this land and together, he and Mair cater to everybody's needs with very comfortable bed and breakfast accommodation provided within the farmhouse itself and three well-equipped self-catering properties available in the farm grounds. All are beautifully decorated and furnished, with The Carthouse boasting the additional feature of a lovely spiral staircase. The heated outdoor swimming pool is a popular attraction and on rainy days, the games room provides alternative entertainment.

We stayed on the B4333, making a diversion to **Cwmduad** and discovered standing in the heart of the village, **Neuadd Wen**, a delightful licensed country guest house well-deserving of its Welsh Tourist Board 3-Crown rating. Although only built some fifteen years ago, the house looks much older than it actually is and features original beams preserved from old derelict farmhouses. There are seven superior letting rooms, six en-suite and all equipped and decorated to a very high standard. Downstairs there are two lounges, one for reading and relaxing in peace, the other with a colour television for your entertainment. The smell of homecooked food will have your nostrils twitching and all meals are provided if required with evening meals a must. With children welcome and a babysitting service available, you really have all you need.

Neuadd Wen, Cwmduad 0267 87438 Map Ref: 5C

Looking like a view from a picture postcard, **Fferm-y-Felin** is a delightful 18th century farm set in the tiny village of Llanpumsaint on the main A485. A leafy lane leads to this beautifully refurbished farmhouse, which has a magnificent lounge so large that there is a fireplace at either end!

Fferm-y-Felin, Llanpumsaint 0267 253498 Map Ref: 5C

Here, original exposed stone walls blend comfortably with pink velvet sofas and a lovely old walnut piano, enhancing an air of quiet relaxation. Children are most welcome and you can choose to stay in the farmhouse or try self-catering in the cottage and converted outbuilding. David, a keen conservationist has also created a beautiful lake which is a haven for various wildfowl, just one of the many attractions at this superlative establishment.

If, as we did, you make your way to **Bronwydd Arms Station**, about three miles outside Carmarthen, you will find yourself taking a step back in time to the grand era of the steam worked branch lines of the Great Western Railway, for this is the southern terminus of the **Gwili Railway.** realise that the railway is completely staffed by volunteer members of the Gwili Railway Preservation Society. The railway runs alongside the River Gwili in the beautiful Gwili Valley on its 1.6 mile journey, hence its name. A major feature is the fully operational 21-lever signal box which dates back to 1885, but you will find there is plenty to interest you here and by visiting, you are helping to preserve this marvellous piece of living history.

Celebrating fifteen years of operation this year, it is amazing to realise that the railway is completely staffed by volunteer members of the Gwili Railway Preservation Society. The railway runs alongside the River Gwili in the beautiful Gwili Valley on its 1.6 mile journey, hence its name. A major feature is the fully operational 21-lever signal box which dates back to 1885, but you will find there is plenty to interest you here and by visiting, you are helping to preserve this marvellous piece of living history.

Gwili Railway, Bronwydd Arms Station
0267 230666 / 0656 73217 Map Ref : 5C

A member of the Welcome Host Scheme and awarded a One Crown classification by the Welsh Tourist Board, **Bryncene Farm** is a working farm where hosts Carol and Keith Burrows encourage guests to get involved. To get here take the Gwili Railway sign off the main A484, travelling through Bronwydd Arms village towards Pontarsais and take the first left after Hollybrook Inn and Bryncene Farm is the second property on the right. This lovely 200 year old farmhouse provides wonderful accommodation for non-smokers in three spacious guest rooms, with the use of cots and highchairs available and excellent homecooking served morning and evening. Wandering through the beautiful farmland, you will meet Carol and Keith's extended family ranging from 'Baby', the friendly bull, to soft cuddly rabbits and chicks, leaving you with memories you will treasure.

Bryncene Farm, Bronwydd Arms 0267 253553 Map Ref : 5C

We stayed on the minor roads,by passing Carmarthen and made our way towards **Llandeilo**, pleased by the rural routes we had taken thus far and not disappointed by our decision to continue this way. Situated on the **B4300** Carmarthen to Llandeilo road, **Capel Uchaf Farm** dates back in parts some five hundred years, and was once the home of a wealthy landowner with many hundreds of acres adjoined to it.

Capel Uchaf Farm, Capel Dewi 0267 290799 Map Ref : 4D

Over the past six years, hard work and sympathetic refurbishment has restored it to its former grand self and it now provides superb accommodation in three beautifully furnished en-suite guest rooms.

The character of the property is enhanced by original features such as exposed wooden lintels and in the breakfast/dining room a huge stone inglenook fireplace. Polished wooden floorboards go hand in hand with period furniture, but are complemented by modern facilities for maximum comfort. Coupled with excellent homecooked food and lovely hosts, Capel Uchaf is a very special holiday base.

Close to **Capel Dewi**, just off the A40 and enjoying a peaceful location on the banks of the River **Cothi** in the centre of **Pontargothi**, yet only ten miles from the M4 motorway, **The Cothi Bridge Hotel** is a convenient and attractive holiday base. Over 100 years old, this impressive establishment has been run for the past two and a half years by Sandie and Huw Jones whose hard efforts and sheer determination have turned it into one of the premier hotels in the area. Beautifully decorated throughout, there are thirteen well-equipped and tastefully furnished en-suite guest rooms each with that individual personal touch. The restaurant is excellent, offering an extensive and varied menu and the friendly relaxed atmosphere created by your welcoming hosts, makes this somewhere you are sure to return.

The Cothi Bridge, Pontargothi 0267 290251 Map Ref : 5D

Continuing on the B4300 is an interesting circuit as you pass by **Paxton Tower,** built in 1811 by Sir William Paxton in honour of Nelson and if nothing else fine views can be had from its view point. On the other side of the river lie the remains of the Welsh **Dryslwyn Castle**, the victim of undermining when beseiged in the 13th century indirectly contributing to its present condition. Continuing you will shortly pass the mansion **Golden Grove,** part of a college but originally built to replace a building burnt down in 1769. In that mansion Jeremy Taylor, a writer and Divine Royalist, took refuge during the Civil War and whilst there wrote many works including

'Golden Grove'. After the mansion you'll soon find yourself seeing **Dynevor Old Castle,** now part of a National Trust Park but with a long tradition and history.

The Old Castle stands on the site of an Iron Age fort, the princedom of Deheubarth was ruled from here. Legend has it too that Merlin's grave is in the area. Rhys ap Gruffydd is thought to have built the first stone castle here in the 12th century. Seen as an important target the castle was under constant seige until the arrival of Edward 1. The Park was recently acquired by the National Trust and is being restored to something of the glory it once had when landscaped in 1775 by 'Capability' Brown. Nearby **Newton House,** privately owned, dates from the 17th century, an earlier 15th century manor having replaced the Old Castle as a place of residence for the Rhys family.

Taking a more circular route towards Llandileo we had the opportunity to visit some places, the first situated two miles from the A40, **Felingwm Pottery** enjoys a roadside location on the **B4310** between **Nantgaredig** and **Brechfa** and is surrounded by the unspoilt beauty of the Cloidach Valley.

Felingwm Pottery, Felingwm 0267 88489 Map Ref : 5D

Ann and Malcolm Griffiths are experienced potters who established Felingwm Pottery some 25 years ago. Within their workshop they produce a superb range of majolica as well as beautiful screen printed bone china and earthenware. They can even supply you with a personalised item for that special occasion, whether a one-off for somebody's birthday, or a hundred pieces for a school celebration. The shop is a browser's paradise with beautifully decorated pieces providing perfect mementos of your visit and the 'seconds' represent remarkable value, with flaws that are often barely visible.

From Brechfa on minor road or just five miles off the A40 from the

Paxton Tower.

junction with the **B4297** heading north to the picturesque village of **Llanfynydd** you will find **Troedyrhiw**, a delightful 18th century Welsh farmhouse set in 8 acres of grounds in a peaceful sheltered valley. Owners Pam and Ken Moore enthusiastically share their charming home with their many guests. The character of this historic house is enhanced by the cosy guest rooms and the three en-suite bedrooms which have every modern facility and comfort, all being furnished attractively in country house style. Guests can enjoy a full English breakfast complete with Ken's legendary Llymru and indulge in an excellent English, Welsh and Continental four-course dinner complemented by fine wine. A vineyard is being planted on the slopes of the valley whilst pedigree Jacob sheep graze the meadows. Pam and Ken can advise on a wealth of spectacular walks (walking sticks provided), castles, fishing and wildlife. As one of the many guests recorded in the Visitors Book, "Back for another visit and it gets better each time; lovely and peaceful; even the Queen couldn't complain!"

Troedyrhiw, Llanfynydd 0558 668792 Map Ref; 5D

Lovers of self-catering will discover a real gem at **Sannan Court**, a former Victorian vicarage and adjacent lodge which lie in the heart of the peaceful village of Llanfynydd. The vicarage, Sannan House, has been sympathetically converted to provide five excellently equipped, self-contained apartments each sleeping four, whilst Sannan Lodge also sleeps four and boasts a magnificent 45ft x 21ft lounge with feature central fireplace and a dining space for up to ten. Additional facilities include a laundry room and drying cabinets, but the real jewel in the crown, is Sannan Court's outstanding salmon and sea trout fishing on 14 miles of the Afon Twyi, making this a haven for the fishing enthusiast.

Sannan Court, Llanfynydd 0656 863606 Map Ref ; 5D

Offering a taste of all that is Welsh, healthy and peaceful, a holiday at **"The Manse"** in **Capel Isaac** can only leave you happy, relaxed and refreshed. About half a mile after the Post Office in Capel Isaac village, turn left and you will find "The Manse" on your right. This former vicarage built one hundred years ago is now a working Organic farm surrounded by spectacular scenery with many places of interest to visit in the area. Run by Tony and Lota Smith, it features rare breed animals and a river, stream and small wood can all be found within the five acres of grounds.

The Manse, Capel Issac 0558 668873 Map Ref ; 6D

The beehives on the farm ensure a good supply of real natural Welsh honey on the breakfast table and for sale. Lota's cooking makes mealtimes a real treat and all the various marmalades, jams, chutneys and pickles are homemade. Most of the food used is home or locally produced. "The Manse" is open all year and registered with the Welsh

Tourist Board is classified as Commended and has been awarded Two Crowns. No smoking. A map of the final approach from the main A40 road to "The Manse" will be supplied on request when booking.

Llandeilo, a small market town that serves the rich farmland surrounding it, is close to several places of interest that make worthwhile diversions whilst in the area. Our first journey was along the B4302 to **Talley Abbey.** Founded in the 12th century by Rhys ap Gruffyd for Premonstratensian canons, who ejected by the Cistercians had appealed to the Archibisop of Canterbury and were granted their religious rights. Parts of the abbey tower, knaves and cloisters are some of the few surviving remains yet there is an air of peace and tranquillity hanging over the ruins. You can make your way to the lakes which the Abbey is named after for a pleasant walk in this attractive location.

To the south east of Llandeilo another place of historical interest is **Carreg Cennen Castle.** Its location on a 300 foot limestone crag which overlooks the river Cennen is quite dramatic and likely to conjure up romantic visions for the visitor. The path up is fairly rigorous but the reward of the remains and the views of the Brecon Beacon National Park and Black monutains worth the effort. The present remains date from the 13th century but there had been a fortress here before that. Tradition has it that the castle was once occupied by Urien, a knight of Arthurs Round Table. The castle was ruined in 1462 being considered a place for bandits, by William Herbert of Raglan. The remains are fairly however, substantial and moved Dylan Thomas to refer to it in some of his work as " Carreg Cennen, King of Time." Being there one could almost agree with his sentiments.

Just outside Llandeilo situated on the A40 at **Rhosmaen, The Plough Inn** is renowned for its warm welcome, superb cuisine and first class accommodation. Run by friendly hosts Giulio and Diane Rocca for the past 24 years, considerable refurbishment has developed this former farmhouse into the outstanding establishment it is today. All twelve beautifully furnished, en-suite guest rooms are named after mythical characters and are equipped to the highest standards ensuring maximum comfort. Five on the ground floor are accessible to wheelchair users. In the comfort of the Towy Lounge you can relax with a drink and choose from an extensive bar menu. Alternatively, the à la carte restaurant is a popular venue with residents and non-residents alike and provides the finest fresh local produce imaginatively prepared to tempt the most discerning palate.

We continued our journey by following a circular route via the Black Mountains towards **Llandovery.** The A476 took us through

The Plough Inn, Rhosmaen 0558 823431 (Fax: 0558 823969)
Map Ref :5F

Llandybie and **Ammanford**,two towns that developed along with the growth of the coalfields. From Ammanford we followed the A474 until the junction with the **A4069** at **Glanaman.** This road took us in a northerly direction over the **Black Mountains.** Looking out west the Tywi Valley drops away from the monutains and we could see Carreg Cennen Castle in the distance.To the east of the road the wild,windswept tops of the 1987 feet of **Foel Fraith** and the ridge of **Bannau Sir Gaerfryddin** ridge in the distance. Part way along the road there is a viewpoint from where you can contemplate the weather beaten landscape and further along a picnic site.

The road eventually arrives at **Llangadog,** a small town which once boasted a castle and now has as its only remains a mound by the village. The castle was destroyed by its owners in 1277, preferring that than the alternative of the castle falling into English hands. **Carn Goch,** the largest hillfort in Wales lies about three miles to the south of Llangadog, its stone ramparts and earthworks covering roughly fifteen acres.

Whilst in the **Llanwrda** area we visited **Felin Newydd** is one of the last working watermills in Wales, fully restored thanks to the intensive conservation efforts of its owners, Malcolm and Wendy Beeson. Situated on the A482 Llanwrda to Lampeter road at the junction with the **B4302** and enjoying a peaceful, rural location in the beautiful Annell Valley, a trip here will take you back in time to a bygone era. You can watch the miller producing stone-ground flour exactly as it would have been produced centuries ago, and follow his fascinating conducted tour. The mill workshop will have you enthralled with its daily demonstrations of traditional crafts such as woodturning

Talley Abbey or Carreg Cennen Castle.

and quilting. Outside you can enjoy Felin Newydd's tranquil surroundings, strolling by the wildlife pond before making your way to the tearoom for some welcome homecooked refreshment.

Felin Newydd, The Mill at Crugybar, Llanwrda 05585 375
Map Ref : 5F

Horse lovers are in for a real treat when they take a riding holiday at **Erw Wen Farm** in **Harford**. To discover this 'hidden' gem, follow the A482 through **Pumpsaint,** eventually crossing the River Twrch then up the hill past the Royal Oak. Half a mile further on turn right at the sign for the farm and continue for about a mile. Shirley Keyte, the friendly proprietor here, has 36 years experience in riding tuition and is a member of various recognised bodies including the British Horse Society. You will find your time here filled with beautiful countryside hacks and treks, longer trips incorporating picnic or pub lunches. With room for ten guests, the atmosphere in the farmhouse is one of friendly bonhomie, everyone living together like one big family and in addition to many other exciting events, you can compete in the end-of-week showjumping competition.

Erw Wen Farm, Harford, Llanwrda 055 85 457 Map Ref : 5F

Llandovery, means 'Church amid the waters' as it stands at the confluence of the Bran, Gwydderig and Twyi. Evidence suggests that the area has been of some importance since Roman times,the church has Roman tiles within its fabric. Rhys Pritchard,known for his preaching and the author of,' The Welshman's Candle ' a collection of verses lived here in the 17th century. So too in the 18th century did William Williams ,a revivalist and hymn writer. A castle once stood on a mound by the cattle market and the town is dotted with pleasant architecture such as the 19th century Market Hall.

Before we leave this area and chapter we made another excursion along a minor road to **Llyn Brianne.** The road passes by the attractive **Dolauhirion Bridge**,a single arched construction spanning the Twyi,built in 1173 by William Edwards. You'll pass close to **Cilycwm**,where the 15th century church contains old wall paintings and the chapel is said to have been the first meeting place of Methodists in Wales. Further along you'll arrive by **Twm Shon Catti's Cave**,the hideout of a 16th century outlaw whose exploits earned him the title as the Robin Hood of Wales. Finally Llyn Brianne lies before you, a reservoir created in the 1970's and in the midst of some beautiful scenery. The water supplies Swansea but the visitor can enjoy the surroundings on trails, from picnic sites. The breeding sites of the rare kite are located in the area but are kept secret due to the threat to this bird.

The road skirts the reservoir and also into our next chapter. After our journey along the coast of Cardigan Bay and into the rich,fertile farmland of Dyfed had gradually begun to give us a foretaste of South Powys. We looked forward to our next discoveries of 'hidden places' in South Powys with its lakes in the north and fine walking country in the south hoping but almost certain that they would match the delightful places we had already found.

CHAPTER FIVE

South Powys.

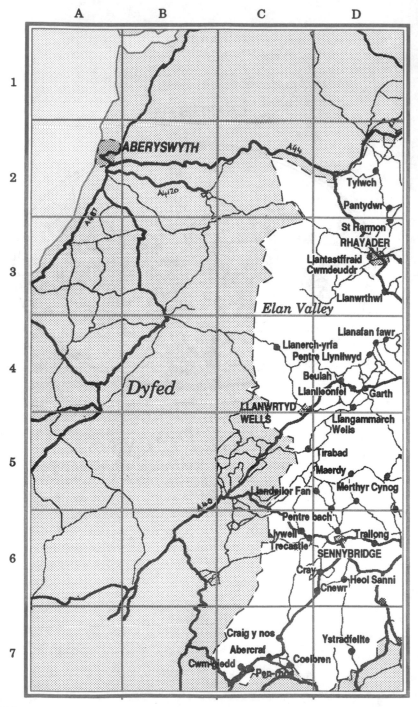

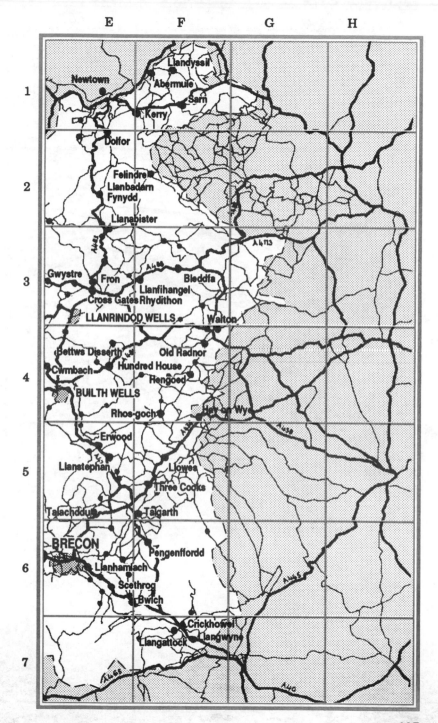

Myndd Epynt Moorland.

CHAPTER FIVE

South Powys.

Places with names, such as **Llandrindod Wells, Brecon, Bronllys**, sounding like strange bedfellows with others like **Hay -on-Wye** or **Crickhowell,** reflect the meeting of two cultures in this border are. It is debatable as to whether the the Welsh and the English will ever see eye to eye on all things but the inroads made into each others 'world' made this part of our journey all the more interesting. The struggle over the centuries for land,power and influence have resulted in a mixture that has left its mark in this area. We'd already passed by some of the Brecon Beacons and Black Mountains so looked forward to more contrasting scenery,places of interest and good walking as we entered into this area

Continuing along the same minor road we were on in the last chapter, past the reservoir Llyn Briane,we turned south along the old drovers road to **Abergwesyn,** in the direction of **Llanwrtyd Wells.** For part of the way the road follows the River Irfon and beside it, picnic sites and trails courtesy of the Forestry Commission. As we came closer to Llantryd Wells, **Mynydd Eppynt,** a remote area of moorland parts of which are used by the Ministry of Defence came into view. Fleetingly our hearts sank, the thought momentarily dashing our expectations by abruptly returning us to the present. Our journey to 'hidden places' had thus far also included an education into the past - perhaps at times through a romantic haze but informative none the less - it seemed a pity to be suddenly reminded of the existence and necessity of a military presence even in todays world.

Gladly it was only a temporary abberation in our journey as we continued on the short distance to Llanwrtyd Wells. The town was once a spa, the curative properties of the sulphur and chalybeate spring waters here discovered by a Reverend Theophilus Evans in 1792,a scurvy sufferer. The consequence of this being that the town has many facilites to make it an ideal attraction during a country holiday. The **Cambrian Welsh Tweed Factory** (Tel: 05913 211) can be found here, where you can observe the production of tweed and then take the opportunity to purchase some of their products from the factory shop.

Should you wish to stay in the area then it would be hard to imagine a more spectacular setting for a holiday than that of **Cwmirfon Lodge** which lies in the heart of the **Irfon Valley,** probably the most beautiful in all Wales, and just three miles from Llanwrtyd Wells. With over three acres of splendid grounds and boasting two and a half miles of private fishing on the River Irfon, this is the charming home of Andrew and Sheila Swindale who offer first class hospitality to their many guests. Beautifully furnished throughout, the Lodge provides accommodation in two lovely, en-suite guest rooms and during the year Sheila and Andrew host regular Rubber Bridge Weekends. Alternative accommodation of an equally high standard is provided in five self-contained cottages which sleep between two and four people.

Cwmirfon Lodge, Llanwrtyd Wells 05913 217 Map Ref ; 4C

We took a minor road to **Llangammarch Wells,** sitting pleasantly at the meeting of the Irfon and Cammarch rivers it made us feel guilt for any prior doubts we had about the area. This, the smallest of Welsh spas, was renowned for its waters containing barium chloride, believed helpful for heart and rheumatic complaints. The village was the birthplace of John Penry (in 1559) a Puritan writer who was hung in London in 1593 after being found guilty of treason. The grandson of Reverend Evans the discoverer of the waters at Llanwrtyd Wells, also named Theophilus, who wrote 'View of the Primitve Age' a classic historical interpretation of the area, was vicar in the village.

Builth Wells, lying by the Wye which is spanned by a six arched bridge, is another town that owes much of its characteristics to once being a fashionable spa. Builths bearing is the opposite to what you might expect when realise that in Welsh history it has earned the nickname,' traitors of Bu-allt '. So called because of the towns refusal to shelter Llewelyn the Last in 1282 from the English, perhaps in spite because over twenty years earlier in 1260, he had partly destroyed the

Builth Wells.

castle. He later died in nearby **Cilmeri.** The Castle mound is all that remains of the stone castle started by Edward 1 but later destroyed.

You would be hard put to find a more picturesque or idyllic location than that of **Caer Beris Manor** which lies just outside Builth Wells on the banks of the River Wye. Originally the site of an Iron Age fort, this lovely Elizabethan style Manor House, once the home of Lord Swansea, is set in 27 acres of beautiful wooded parkland, offering wonderful views and secluded walks. There are twenty two beautifully furnished en-suite guest rooms and the oak panelled dining room provides an elegant setting for a superb gourmet menu and fine wine list which have a worldwide reputation. With numerous activities available, including fishing, pony trekking and shooting, you have all you need for that relaxing break away.

Caer Beris Manor, Builth Wells 0982 552601 (Fax: 0982 552586)
Map Ref ; 4E

We decided to head towards the Welsh Lake District, the **Elan Valley and Claerwen Reservoirs.** Taking the **A470** we passed through **Llanelwedd,** home of Royal Welsh Agricultural Society Showground where its main event is held in July each year. The road follows the Wye as it flows energetically down the valley until you reach **Newbridge -on- Wye.** A popular centre for anglers and also the place where you'll find the **Mid Wales House Gallery,** an art and craft shop. Two miles further on and you'll pass by **Doldowlod House,** once the home of James Watt the engineer.

We made our way through this lovely valley, ideal for walkers and part of the **Wye Valley Walk** to **Elan Village** where a Visitor Centre (Tel:- 0597 810898) has information on this area of reservoirs. The Elan reservoirs, a string of five dammed lakes together roughly nine miles long, were constructed from 1892 - 96 and the Claerwen, four miles long and completed in 1952, supply water to Birmingham. Before the flooding the Elan Valley was renowned for its wildness and
202

beauty. Following the road from the village you arrive at the **Garreg Ddu Viaduct** which if you cross and continue on by the shore of the Caben Coch, passes by the spot where **Nant Gwyllt** lies, the house where Shelley and his wife Harriet stayed in 1812. Apparently when the water is low,the walls to the garden are exposed to view. The house itself inspired the novelist,Francis Brett Young,to write ' The House under the Water '. Taking a northerly direction from the viaduct you pass the spot where **Cwm Elan** - the house Shelly stayed at after his expulsion from Oxford in 1811 - is submerged.

We continued on our journey passing through **Rhayader**, its name meaning 'Waterfall of the Wye' which the town stands above. The falls have all but disappeared with the construction of the bridge in 1780. The town does have some claim to fame in that Rebecca Riots took place here during the 19th century. Men dressed as women, nicknamed 'Rebecca's Daughters' destroyed turnpikes in protest of the high toll charges. Nowadays the town is a market centre,known for its sheep fairs and also popular as a holiday centre for country lovers with the opportunity for walking,fishing and pony trekking in the surrounding area. Here you'll also find **Gigrin Farm** where you can visit a working hill farm and watch its operation along the farm trail.

Along the **A44** from Rhayader you'll pass through **Crossgates** from where a short excursion northwards will take you to the remains of **Cwmhir Abbey** in the **Clywedog Valley**. Founded in 1143 for Cistercians it was twice destroyed in its history. Firstly by Henry 111 in 1231 and again in 1402 by Owain Glyndwr who thought the monks to be English in disguise. By Dissolution the Abbey was home to only three monks but despite the few remains the body of Llewelyn the Last is thought to have been buried here in 1282 after his death at Cilmeri. Today a blackthorn marks the spot where his remains are believed to lie.

From Crossgates it is but a short distance to **Llandrindod Wells**, its spacious Edwardian style a hangover from its days as a fashionable spa town. The towns popularity as a spa boomed with the development of the railway,a popularity which was to continue until the 1930's. At its peak some 80,000 visitors came to try its sulphur waters with its curative properties. Although only a scattered hamlet until a hotel was built in 1749,whence it developed, for a time, a reputation as the haunt of gamblers and rakes the town does have older historical roots. The Romans had a fort at nearby **Castell Collen** and the **Church of Trinity** dates from the 12th century.

The **Llandrindod Museum** (Tel:- 0597 824513) contains many finds from the Roman fort and in the same street you'll find

Automobile Palace (Tel:- 0597 822214). There visitors can view the Tom Norton collection of bicycles and tricycles from 1867 to 1938. At **Rock Park Spa,** (0597 824307) you can try the water that made Llandrindod famous at the 19th century Pump Room.

Back on the A44 we headed east round the southern reaches of moorland and the **Radnor Forest** stopping at **Llanfihangel -nant-Melan** to view the waterfall ' **Water -Breaks -its- Neck** ' falling through the ravine. You can take a pleasant walk on the top of the ravine and for the ambitious paths lead through Radnor Forest to **Llanfihangel Rhydithon** and **Bleddfa.**

New Radnor once the county town of Radnorshire, has a motte and bailey that originates from the 11th century and like many other castles in the border area suffered under various hands. It was destroyed by King John,rebuilt by Henry 111 and again destroyed by Owain Glyndwr in 1401. The castle also claims to be the starting point of Archibishop Baldwins travels through Wales to preach of the Third Crusade.

In tranquil village of New Radnor, just past the central monument that you will find **The Eagle Hotel.** Extensive refurbishment has now provided half of the eight guest rooms with en-suite facilities

The Eagle Hotel, Broad Street, New Radnor 0544 21208 Map Ref ; 4F

and the restaurant has a large local following, due to its excellent menu of fresh local produce which includes salmon, trout and game when in season. There are also separate vegetarian and children's menus and a wonderful choice of desserts. The views from here are stunning and coffee on the patio terrace is a real treat. During 1993, the hotel is opening an Art and Crafts Centre plus developing a splendid range of activity holidays, such as canoeing, pony trekking, climbing and paragliding.

Old Radnor, some two miles further along was once home to King

Llandridod Wells.

Harold whom, as we all know, was killed at Hasting in 1066. The motte by the church was the site of his castle and the church itself contains interesting examples of 14th century building.

Following the border and Offa's Dyke Path we made our way along the **B4594** passing through small hamlets with odd names such as **Michaelchurch on Arrow** until we came to **Painscastle.** Sometimes know as Castell Paen, this early Norman motte is associated with the notorious William de Braose. The castle was put under seige by Gwenwyn-wyn of Powys,unsucessfully, when seeking revenge for his cousin who had been captured by De Braose, who after dragging him by a horses tail to Brecon subsequently executed him.

We then cut across to **Clyro**,where once the Romans had a station and there are some remains of a motte and bailey built by De Braose. The 19th century diarist Francis Kilvert was curate here from 1865 - 72 recording village life and that of the surrounding countryside.

Close by **Hay -on- Wye,** on the banks of the river and just in Wales is known for its market that serves the area and its large second hand book businesses carried out from the many shops in the town. A Roman presence was here,there are traces of a fort across the river and the Normans a motte and bailey. This was replaced by a a stone castle that was in the hands of the De Braose family and as with others was destroyed by Glyndwr in the early 1400's.

Cockalofty Hill Farm, Caecilalltddu, Llanifon 0497 821100 Map Ref; 5E

Cockalofty is a real retreat set in splendid isolation on the upland landscape of the Brecon Beacons National Park. Caecilalltddu, its real Welsh name, means 'Enclosure-by-the-spring-on-the-slopes-of-the-Black-Mountains'! It is 1000ft above Hay-on-Wye which, surprisingly, is only 4 miles down the road abuzz with 30 bookshops, literary and cultural and market day activities.You may walk the undulating terrain of Cockalofty itself to admire the views, the orchids, and special flock of Black Welsh Mountain sheep; or venture

206

Hay -on- Wye.

further, amongst wild ponies and skylarks, to the higher peaks of the Black Mountains just 2 miles away, refreshing yourself with the clean Cockalofty air.

Glasbury was once the site of a Roman station and in the heart of the ancient village of which lies in a bend of the river Wye, you will discover a tranquil holiday haven at **The Forge**, the lovely home of Jo Northam. This charming country cottage dates back to the 17th century and is beautifully furnished in keeping with its age and character. There is a choice of breakfast each morning and accommodation is provided in four very comfortable guest rooms, one of which is en-suite. A warm, welcoming atmosphere pervades throughout and the presence of ducks, bantams and pheasants in the lovely garden merely enhances the country feel so that you can't help but relax.

The Forge, Glasbury, Near Hay-on-Wye 0497 847237 Map Ref ; 5f

Just a mile or so away in **Felindre** village, just down from the Three Horseshoes pub, stands a truly wonderful 'hidden place', **Old Gwernyfed Country Manor**. Approaching this impressive Grade I listed Elizabethan Manor down a long drive, it may well seem familiar, since it has featured in various TV programmes. Built during the 1600s, this was the Manor House of the area where Charles I stayed in 1645 and today, thanks to the loving care and hard work of owners, Dawn and Roger Beetham, it provides unique and grand accommodation, retaining many original features including a Minstrel's Gallery, Priest's hiding hole and "acres" of ancient oak panelling, whilst offering every modern comfort. Despite the grandeur of your surroundings, the atmosphere is immediately warm and welcoming. Each room is different in both shape and design and the 11 bedrooms are individually named. Nine have en-suite bathroom and all are exquisitely furnished in keeping with the age and character of the building. The elegant dining room with its vast 12' fireplace, provides the perfect setting for Dawn's substantial breakfast and mouthwatering dinner menus. Leaving here revitalised and refreshed, your only problem will be making your way back to 'the real world'!

Old Gwernyfed Country Manor, Felindre, Three Cocks 0497 847376
Map Ref ; 5F

Idyllically set in the historic grounds of **Bronllys Castle** on the banks of the River Llynfi, the **Alex Williams Collection** can be found in a lovely old country house situated on the north eastern boundary of the Brecon Beacons National Park six and a half miles from Hay-on-Wye. Alex Williams is well known for his paintings of the border countryside showing much-loved depictions of farm animals and poultry and glimpses into life on the river bank. Alex welcomes visitors to view by appointment, a permanent but always changing exhibition of his paintings and other work which is available in the gallery and well stocked pottery shop on the premises.

The Alex Williams Collection, Bronllys 0874 711826
(Fax 0874 71185) Map Ref ; 5E

Only two and a half miles from the Breconshire Black Mountains, peaceful and secluded yet within walking distance of Bronllys and the small market town of Talgarth, this is an ideal centre for both activity or more leisurely pursuits. The centrally heated, self catering accommodation is comfortable and well equipped. One of the apartment houses a three quarter size snooker table and is also suitable for semi-ambulant wheelchair users. Highly approved. Open every day of the year.

Situated on the hillside above a bubbling stream and sheltered by the mountains, a mile off the A470 Brecon-Builth Wells road, close to Bronllys you will discover a lovely 300 year old farmhouse. **Cilfodig Farm** is the delightful home of Phyllis Evans who provides comfortable accommodation in three spacious bedrooms. The garden is full of butterflies and herbaceous borders, with three mature walnut trees on the drive beside the stream and it would be hard to imagine a better setting for a 'get-away-from-it-all' break. Staying here you will be well fed, since Phyllis is an excellent cook and readily provides an evening meal by prior arrangement. Alternatively, you can stay in Phyllis's fully-equipped self-catering cottage which lies further down the valley and makes an ideal holiday base.

Cilfodig Farm, Llandefalle 0874 754207 Map Ref ; 5E

Talgarth is a market town that once stood in the midst of the Norman drive into Wales and still retains some defensive characteristics of those times. It is also associated with Hywel Harris a Methodist revivalist who established a religious community 'The Connexion' at Trefecca House in 1752. It is now a college that has a museum containing many rare books published by the community.

Talgarth has many historic associations with famous figures such as St. Gwendoline and Sir William Vaughan, the first Sheriff of Breconshire. More recently however, Talgarth has been temporarily invaded by a BBC TV film crew. Talgarth was found to be the perfect location in which to shoot 'Morgan's Boy', a recent television series.

Pat Banford is proprietor of the **Olde Masons Arms Hotel**, an inn that dates as far back as the 16th century and some people believe even earlier. Run as a small country hotel, Pat has taken great pains to ensure the building has retained much of its original style and character. We found our room very comfortable, with the added joy of an en-suite bathroom and tea and coffee making facilities.

The restaurant serves an excellent à la carte menu. You may chose from a wide range of dishes which included steak au poivre, veal cordon bleu, chicken chasseur and breaded plaice. There is an open fire in the lounge bar for those cooler evenings. A bar menu is available as well, with something to suit all tastes. Well worth a visit, we found The Olde Mason's Arms Hotel a peaceful and very pretty place.

The Olde Masons Arms, Talgarth 0874 711688 Map Ref ; 5F

For first class farmhouse accommodation in idyllic surroundings, non-smokers need look no further than **Upper Trewalkin**, the charming 15th century home of Mrs. Meudwen Stephens.

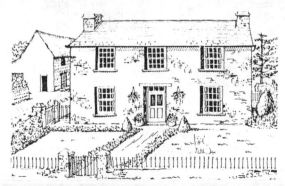

Upper Trewalkin Pengenffordd, Near Talgarth 0874 711349 Map Ref ; 6E

Bronllys Castle.

Lying a mile out of Pengenffordd, it is set within beautiful gardens and surrounded by breathtaking views, making it a simply wonderful touring base. Beautifully furnished throughout, there is a warm, welcoming atmosphere and farmhouse style antiques enhance the character of this lovely house. There are three spacious guest rooms, each with en-suite facilities and downstairs the separate dining room and sitting room both have a log-burning stove which lends a snug air on chilly evenings. Mrs. Stephens is a superb cook and has even appeared on television, so dining here is a delight, both at breakfast and dinner.

Situated behind the splendid village church in Llanfilo, a short distance from Talgarth off the **A438,** you will find a lovely holiday base at the Old Rectory, an impressive Georgian fronted house, parts of which date back some 400 years. This is the charming home of Mrs Dene Thomas, who enjoys sharing it with her many guests and offers the best in friendly Welsh hospitality. The house is built into the hillside on split levels, with a delightful sun terrace to the rear which is reached via the first floor and offers stunning views across the valley to the Black Mountains. There are three well-equipped and very comfortable guest rooms and well-behaved dogs are welcome. In addition to a choice of Continental or full English breakfast, a wholesome evening meal can be provided by prior arrangement.

The Old Rectory, Llanfilo, Brecon 0874 711237 Map Ref ; 6E

Llangorse Lake, roughly four miles from Talgarth is about four miles in circumference and the second largest natural lake in Wales after Bala. Today it is used for water sports but traces have been found of a prehistoric lake dwelling,considered to be the food of the legend of a drowned settlement here. Situated on the **B4560**, a mile from Llangorse on the Talgarth Road, **Trewalter House** is the charming home of Jean and Peter Abbott who enjoy sharing it with their many guests. The warm welcome you receive on your arrival is

Llangorse Lake.

followed by friendly, personal service throughout your stay and the three en-suite guest rooms are beautifully furnished and provide every modern facility for maximum comfort. An optional four-course evening meal is provided and the residential licence means you can complement Jean's excellent cooking with a choice bottle of wine if you wish. With beautiful walking country all around and many local attractions within easy reach, Trewalter House makes an ideal touring base, worthy of its Three Crown Highly Commended award from the Wales Tourist Board.

Trewalter House, Llangorse 087 484 442 Map Ref ; 6E

We turned back into Powys deciding to leave the south eastern part of this area to the latter part of this chapter and made our way to **Brecon.** Lying at the meeting point of the rivers Usk and Honddu this town has old origins. The remains of the Roman fort at **Y Gaer** some three miles west of town are tangible evidence of the areas early history. First built circa 75 and having two rebuilds before being abandoned around 290. In its time the fort garrisoned the 2nd Legion and the Vettonian Spanish cavalry. Parts were excavated by Sir Mortimer Wheeler in 1924 and you can see parts of the outer wall,in some places as ten feet tall,as well as traces of the gates.

The town grew around the castle built by Bernard of Newmarch in the late 11th century. It was beseiged by Llewelyn the Last and during the Glyndwr rebellion but by the time of the Civil War,the town considered its growing cloth trade to be of more importance and therefore remained neutral -the citizens going as far as pulling down parts of the town walls and castle. Brecon was the birthplace of several people of prominence - Dr Hugh Price (1495-1574) the founder of Jesus College, Oxford; Dr.Thomas Coke (1747-1814) the founder of the American Methodist Episcopalian Church; Sarah Siddons (1755-1831) a celebrated actress from the 18th century and her brother Charles Kemble to mention but a few.

215

The Priory Church of St John the Evangelist, originating from an 11th century cell of the Bendectine monastery of Battle in Sussex was elevated to Cathedral status in 1923. Inside there are many interesting examples of religious artefacts and by the aisles once full with Chapels dedicated to crafts people only that to Corvisors (shoemakers) remains.

The **Brecknock Museum,**close to Captains Walk - so called because it was used to exercise captured French Officers - is a fascinating place to visit.(Tel:- 0874 4121) Its exhibits are concerned mainly with local history which help give a greater insight into the area. If hungry for more history then you can continue to the **South Wales Borderers Regimental Musuem** which tells of the 280 year history of the regiment and the sixteen Victoria Crosses its men have been awarded in that time.

Hidden away in the heart of Brecon, with its striking flower bedecked Georgian frontage, **The George Hotel** looks out from George Street onto ancient alleyways. This delightful country town hotel is renowned throughout the area for the intimate atmosphere of its restaurant and its friendly lounge bar. All twelve guest rooms are en-suite and have a superior Georgian feel about them which is enhanced by beautiful period furnishings. The service here is impeccable - always friendly and helpful, which makes staying here a real joy. To the rear of the hotel is a delightful garden where you can relax 'al fresco' with a quiet pre-dinner drink before making you way to the aforementioned restaurant. The menu offers a vast selection of French, Welsh and English cuisine prepared to the highest standards, with separate menus for children and vegetarians. Throughout your stay you will find the staff here will do their utmost to cater for your every need, ensuring a relaxing holiday for all.

The George Hotel and Restaurant, Brecon 0874 623422
Map Ref; 6E

Travelling through Brecon town along the A40, about 100 yards after crossing the River Usk bridge you will find the **Beacons Guest House.** Open all year round this beautiful Georgian house has its own private car park and ten very comfortable guest rooms each superbly furnished in keeping with the period and character of the building. Seven have en-suite bath/shower and all provide a hot drinks tray and colour TV. For a treat, why not ask for the master bedroom where the splendid four-poster bed is complemented by a beautifully moulded ceiling and lovely marble fireplace. Beacons is a licensed guest house with its own bar and dining here is a real pleasure. Beacons Restaurant, which is open to non-residents, is "Taste of Wales Recommended" which gives an indication of the first class cuisine you can expect.

Beacons Guest House, Brecon 0874 623339 Map Ref ; 6E

Passing along the southern edges of the Mynydd Eppynt, our earlier dismay finally quashed as the almost mystical,wild land towards the north gave way to hill farms and treelines we made our way to **Sennybridge.** Developed during the 19th century along with the railways as a centre for livestock trading in the area the town still retains that argicultural air.

Cwmcamlais Uchaf Farm, Sennybridge 0874 636376 Map Ref ; 6D

Five miles from Brecon on the Sennybridge road, about a mile into the Camlais Valley, you will find a lovely place to stay at **Cwmcamlais Uchaf Farm.** This is the charming home of Jean and Hywel Phillips, a house filled with laughter and warmth, where guests are treated as welcome friends and spoilt with magnificent homecooked breakfasts. There are three cosy, beautifully furnished bedrooms, one en-suite and two with private facilities. Set within 200 acres of rolling hills in the heart of the Brecon Beacons National Park, with the famous Camlais Waterfalls forming part of their land, this is a place for walking and watching the wealth of bird and animal life.

If you take the turning at Sennybridge towards **Pentrefelin,** just after crossing the Llwyncyntefin Bridge over the River Usk, you will discover **Glynderi Pottery.** This delightful establishment is housed within the former 17th century coach-house stables of Llwyncyntefin Manor and is run by a very gifted and creative lady called Ruth Lyle. Visitors are welcome to browse and watch any work in hand, such as preparing clay, throwing, and glazing. Attractive ranges of domestic and garden pots are displayed in the showroom alongside bells and hand-modelled little animals. There is also a gallery showing larger one-off pots and paintings. Children are encouraged to model clay in an activity area set aside for them. An added attraction of a visit here is the homemade light lunches and cream teas served in the lovely garden or tearoom.

Glynderi Pottery, Sennybridge 0874 636564 Map Ref ; 6D

We headed into the Black Mountains taking a minor road south off the **A4215.** The road follows the Senni through **Heol Senn** before eventually climbing sharply and squeezing its way along the narrow valley between Fan Llia which rises to 2071 feet on the eastside and Fan Nedd 2200 feet on the west. The road now follows the Afon Llia as it increases its pace along the valley and close by where the river passes through woods you'll find a picnic spot. On the other side, just

218

off the road, **Maen Madog**, a nine foot high standing stone has a Latin inscription stating that Dervacus, son of Justus lies here. The stone itself was probably erected around 2000 BC. Sarn Helen, another Roman road joins the road as we eventually enter **Ystradfellte**.

Set high on the edge of the village, bordering open countryside in the heart of the Brecon Beacons National Park, **Maesyronnen** is an attractive architect designed bungalow, where Joan and Caradog Morgan provide very comfortable overnight accommodation.

Maesyronnen, Ystradfellte 0639 722343 Map Ref; 7D

There are two lovely guest rooms with private or en-suite facilities, and the decor throughout is simply lovely. The views on all sides are breathtaking and Joan serves a fabulous breakfast which really sets you up for a day exploring. With dippers on the water, an abundance of fishing and walks nearby and Brecon and Abergavenny within easy reach, Maesyronnen makes a wonderful touring base.

Beyond the village we soon came to **Porth -yr- Ogof**, a delightful area of waterfalls as the river Meltte descends through woodland. There are marked picnic spots and several trails to follow through the woods to view the falls. The road then continues down to **Pontneddfacht** where it meets the **A465** which we took until the A4109 at **Glyn Neath.** Continuing on the A4109 we followed the signs for **Abercraf,** from there taking the **A4067** in a north easterly direction back into Powys. The road follows the river Tawe, waterfalls can be seen by taking minor roads from Abercraf or further up the A4067 at **Pen -y- cae.** However, we were drawn to two places of interest just further up the road. Firstly at **Craig -y- Nos Country Park** its forty acres providing the opportunity for a pleasant day out. The mansion in the grounds was built in 1842 and purchased by the opera singer Adelina Patti in 1878 to share with her second husband, the tenor Nicolini. Here they relaxed between vigorous tours enjoying the surroundings, her aviary, winter garden and performances in the small theatre,a replica of Drury Lane in London, which she had built in 1891.

Close by the **Dan -yr- Ogof Caves** (Tel:- 0639 730284) also makes for an interesting day out. The three show caves were discovered in 1912 and finally opened to the public in the 1960's. The three caves consist of, Dan -yr- Ogof the longest show cave in Britain, the Cathedral the largest and Bone where you can learn something of life in prehistoric times. The showcaves also have a Dinosaur Park, museum and artificial ski slope within the its grounds.

We continued on the A4067 back north to slightly retrace our journey through Powys. As the road enters the pass between the Cefn Cul 1844 feet and the Fan Gyhirych 2381 feet a minor road leads off to the north following the Tawe. Along this road you'll find a prehistoric stone circle, an apparently rare oval shaped of which there are few examples in Britain. The main road passes by Cray reservoir and through moorland where we turned to head back through Heol Senn deciding to pass through the **Mynydd Illtyd Common**. Here you'll find the Brecon Beacons Mountain Centre (Tel:- 0874 3366) which has an information centre and marked picnic spots for you to enjoy the scenery. There are also well as some interesting remains to be seen in the area. **Twyn y Gaer**,a Bronze Age burial chamber and **Bedd Illytd** its modest stones belying the fact that tradition believes it to be the grave of St.Illtyd,the founder of the monastery at Llanwit Major.

Back along the A40 to Brecon we then turned off down the **B4558** to make our way along by part of the Monmouthshire and Brecon Canal. Just beyond **Talybont -on- Usk** the canal passes through the 375 yards of the Ashford Tunnel. Turning at Talybont we made our way through Aber to the **Talybont Reservoir**, in an attractive narrow valley surrounded by forest. From the car park at the far end of the reservoir there are several forest trails and for the energetic a pleasant, if rugged walk,can be started from here. Passing by waterfalls you can follow a footpath along the **Craig y Fan Ddu** ridge to some fine views across the Brecon Beacons. Continuing round on the footpath then turning south you'll pass by a memorial to a Wellington bomber that crashed here in 1941,some of its remains can be see further along the route. Soon you'll arrive at the ' Balcony ' where on a good day you'll be able to see across to the Black Mountains and Sugar Loaf. The route drops down back towards the waterfalls and car park. Should you decide to try this demanding walk,or any other similiar route suggested in the book,it is advisable to check the weather,your clothing and be armed with a good OS map.

Another rigorous walk can be made by following the road from nearby **Llangynidr** up onto the **Myndd LLangynidr.** Across open moorland a footpath will take you close to the **Chartists Cave** where members stored ammunition during their active years during the 19th century. Again should you wish to take this route it is advisable to be cautious it terms of the weather, clothing and so forth.

Tretower in the Usk Valley is known for its Court and Castle. The **Court** is a fine example of a later medieval manor house, its oldest stonework dating from the 14th century. The manor is in complete condition and you'll have the opportunity to admire the masonry and woodwork that went into this structure. **Tretower Castle** was built, as was **Castell Dinas** near Talgarth further north, in this valley to discourage Welsh rebellion but was nontheless beseiged by Llewelyn the Last and almost destroyed by Glyndwr. The 12th century ruins lie across from the manor and are interesting in that the castle was unique in its design of a cylindrical tower within a square keep.

Whilst you are visiting the ancient village of Tretower, you will find the ideal place to stay at **The Firs,** a superbly converted estate cottage and outbuildings situated opposite Tretower Castle. This delightful house is the home of welcoming hostess Mary Eckley, who provides superb accommodation in four beautifully furnished bedrooms, two of which are en-suite, and all reached via a lovely spiral stone stairway. With an à la carte breakfast awaiting you each morning, it comes as no surprise to learn that Mary has earned a Dragon Award, a Welcome Host Award and a 3-Crown Highly Commended rating. With the impressive backdrop of the Black Mountains offering a wealth of beautiful walks, this enchanting part of the Usk Valley must be seen to be believed.

The Firs, Tretower, Crickhowell 0874 730780 Map Ref ; 7F

It is perhaps a mile or two to our last destination **Crickhowell,** sitting between the **Table** and **Sugar Loaf Mountains.** The town gets its name from the hillfort on Table Mountain, **Crug Hywel.** A medieval bridge of thirteen arches, restructured during the 17th century, spans the Usk just outside this town which was the birthplace of Sir George Everest in 1790,the man who gave his name to the

Himalayan mountain that has serious mountaineers drooling at its mention. Just east of the town on the way to Abergavenny a minor road leads part way up Sugar Loaf Mountain and a footpath takes you to the 1955 foot summit. Not quite Everest but wonderful views of the Usk Valley, Black Mountains and beyond all the same.

For a quiet weekend away or a relaxing holiday base, it is hard to imagine a finer setting than that of **Gliffaes Country House Hotel** which lies on the banks of the River Usk just four miles outside Crickhowell. The hotel grounds are an absolute delight and friendly proprietors Sam and Nick Brabner have established a beautiful collection of trees, shrubs and flowering plants, plus lawned areas for putting, croquet and bowls. Nick is a master fisherman and guests here can also enjoy trout, salmon and coarse fishing by arrangement. The hotel is beautifully furnished throughout, with Victorian furniture enhancing the country house atmosphere in the panelled sitting-room and regency-style drawing room. Accommodation is provided in thirty very comfortable en-suite guest rooms, all equipped to a high standard. The elegant dining room has French windows opening onto the terrace with fabulous views all round and provides the perfect setting for the mouthwatering cuisine provided by the table d'hôte and à la carte menus. The accompanying wine list is equally impressive and the introductory words of Aristophanes provide additional incentive, if any were needed, to sample some of the fine vintages offered: "Tis when men drink they thrive, grow wealthy, speed their business, win their suits, make themselves happy, benefit their friends. Go fetch me out a stoup of wine, and let me moisten my wits, and utter something bright."

Gliffaes Country House Hotel, Crickhowell 0874 730371
(Fax: 0874 730463) Map Ref ; 7F

You'll also find in Llangattock, **The Horsehoe Inn,** formerly a 17th century coaching inn now run by Mr and Mrs Groves which retains an ' olde worlde ' atmosphere. Here you can enjoy a selection of fine ales and delicious barsnacks. Alternatively you can eat in the thirty seat restaurant which had a very reasonably priced menu that includes vegetarian choices.Children are welcome in this Inn where overnight accomodation is available with tea/coffee facilties in every room. The Horeshoe's situation makes it an ideal stopping off point to enjoy one of the many outdoor activities that are available in the area.

The Horseshoe Inn, Llangattock 0873 810393 Map Ref ; 7F

Across the river,beyond Llangattock a minor road will lead you to the **Craig -y- Cilau Nature Reserve.** This 157 acre reserve is one of the best in the Brecons with over two hundred and fifty plant species recorded and over fifty kinds of birds breeding within its grounds. A cave system of some twelve miles begins in the reserve but entrance is only for approved caving clubs.

So we draw to an end of our journey in South Wales. For us it has been a journey of enlightenment where our earlier ignorance of this wonderful part of the British Isles has partly been put to right. As with everything there is always more to learn and we hope that ' Hidden Places ' has at least unlocked the door to some of your curiosity even if not answering some of your questions concerning South Wales. As you are probably aware there are vast amount of literature dealing with the areas history,development,characters and so forth. We hope we've pointed you in some of the right directions.

Finally,it should be said that this book would not have been possible without the fine hospitality we received during our visit to South Wales. For this we thank all concerned from the bottom of our hearts for making it a memorable trip. We would hope that should you try any of the places of interest,hotels,pubs,restaurants,tea shops and such that we have included in this book that you mention the fact that ' Hidden Places ' helped you in coming to that choice. In the meantime we wish you a pleasant trip through this often delightful area of South Wales.

Tourist Information Centres.

Aberaeron, The Quay 0545 570602

Aberdulais, Aberdulais Basin, Nr Neath 0639 633531

Abergavenny, Swan Meadow, Cross Street 0873 857588

Aberyswyth, Terrace Road 0970 612125

Barry Island, The Triangle, Paget Road 0446 747171

Borth, High Street 0970 871174

Brecon, Cattle Market Car Park 0874 622485

Builth Wells, Groe Car Park 0982 553307

Careloen, Ffwrrwm Art and Craft Centre, High Street 0633 430777

Cardiff, 8-14 Bridge Street 0222 227281

Cardigan, Theatr Mwldan 0239 613230

Carmarthen, Lammas Street 0267 231557

Chepstow, The Gatehouse, High Street 0291 623772

Ebbw Vale, Garden Festival Wales, Victoria 0495 350198

Fishgaurd, 4 Hamilton Street 0348 873484

Haverfordwest, Old Bridge 0347 763110

Llandovery, Central Car Park, Broad Street 0550 20693

Llandrindod Wells, Old Town Hall, Memorial Gardens 0597 822600

Llanelli, Public Library, Vaughan Street 0554 772020

Llandiloes, Longbridge Street 05512 2605

Merthyr Tydfil, 14a Glebeland Street 0685 79884

Milford Haven, Torch Theatre, St Peters Road 0646 690866

Monmouth, Shire Hall, Agincourt Square 0600 713899

New Quay, Church Street 0545 860865

Newcastle Emlyn, Market Hall 0239 711333

Newport, Newport Museum and Art Gallery, John Frost Square 0633 842962

Penarth, The Esplanade, Penarth Pier 0222 708849

Raglan, Granada Services South, A40, Nr Monmouth 0600 83495

Rhayader, The Old Swan, West Street 0597 810591

Swansea, PO Box 59, Singleton Street, 0792 468321

Tenby, The Croft 0834 2402

Tredegar, Bryn Bach Country Park, Merthyr Road 0495 711816

Town Index

THE HIDDEN PLACES

If you would like to have any of the titles currently available in this series, please complete this coupon and send to:

M & M Publishing Ltd
Tryfan House, Warwick Drive,
Hale, Altrincham, Cheshire, WA15 9EA

	Each	Qty
Somerset, Avon and Dorset	£ 5.90	......
Yorkshire and Humberside	£ 5.90	......
Devon and Cornwall	£ 5.90	......
North Yorkshire	£ 5.90	......
The Lake District	£ 5.90	......
Southern and Central Scotland	£ 5.90	......
Hampshire and the Isle of Wight	£ 5.90	......
The Cotswolds (Gloucestershire & Wiltshire)	£ 5.90	......
Thames and Chilterns	£ 5.90	......
East Anglia (Norfolk & Suffolk)	£ 5.90	......
Lancashire & Cheshire	£ 5.90	......
Hereford & Worcester	£ 5.90	......
Northumberland & Durham	£ 5.90	......
North Wales	£ 5.90	......

Set of any Five   £20.00

Total   £

Price includes Postage and Packing

NAME...

ADDRESS...

....

..............................POST CODE....................................

Please make cheques payable to: M & M Publishing Ltd